Ian Seymour has excelled in sales the hard way. H
began as a teenager when he established his own bus
merchandise door-to-door. Now in his thirties, he has
the world and has made enough from selling to be able to
As well as being in business, he has for many years been invo
in managing and training sales personnel and is now a sough
after speaker at sales-training seminars. *One on One,* his first
book, is based on his own experience in many different areas of
selling. He now lives near London with his wife and family.

ONE ON ONE

The Secrets of Professional Sales Closing

IAN SEYMOUR

PELICAN PUBLISHING COMPANY
Gretna 1996

First published by Corgi Books, Transworld Publishers, Ltd., in Great
    Britain, Australia, and New Zealand, 1994
Published by arrangement with the author by
    Pelican Publishing Company, 1996

First printing, 1994
Second printing, May 1996

*The word "Pelican and the depiction of a pelican are trademarks of
Pelican Publishing Company, Inc., and are registered in the
U.S. Patent and Trademark Office.*

Library of Congress Cataloging-in-Publication Data

Seymour, Ian.
    One on One : the secrets of professional sales closing / Ian
Seymour.
        p.   cm.
    Includes bibliographical references and index.
    ISBN 1-56554-213-4 (alk. paper)
    1. Selling.   2. Sales management.   I. Title.
HF5438.25.S472 1996
658.85—dc20   96-3579
                                                               CIP

Manufactured in the United States of America

Published by Pelican Publishing Company, Inc.
1101 Monroe Street, Gretna, Louisiana 70053

This book is dedicated to the memory of Edith Jones,
with love and affection

CONTENTS

Contents 9

ACKNOWLEDGMENTS

There are many people who made this book possible and my thanks go out to all of them. However, there are a few special people that I would like to acknowledge here. First to Suzanne, Kimberley, Aaron, Ron and Lilly for their love and support. I would like to thank my editor John Saddler, who is a real Pro-Ed if ever there was one, and also Averil Ashfield and Cathy Hopkins. My thanks also go the staff of Active Image for their hours of labour over my manuscript. And finally, a very special thank you to J.C. and two members of his staff at Abacus, who gave me more help than they will ever know in preparing the final text. Thank you all.

INTRODUCTION

Once upon a time, at the beginning of the World, God created salespeople. And the salespeople went forth and multiplied in abundance and they took on all different shapes and sizes and colours. The salespeople flourished and diversified into many different fields and backgrounds and into all walks of life. They took on the roles of executives, sales managers, franchisees, business people, shop-owners and the self-employed, agents, assistants, representatives, consultants, advisers and a special breed of commission only. In short, salespeople. And God saw what he had done, and he was pleased.

One on One: The Secrets of Professional Sales Closing is a book for all those salespeople, and for anyone in business who wants to succeed and grow and prosper. Anyone can sell, but it's closing that makes the sale, and *One on One* will teach you how to do just that – close the sale, day in day out, year after year. This is not a storybook, but a detailed, comprehensive sales closing manual that will show you not just what you should do but exactly how you should do it. Inside these pages you will find time-kept secrets, and techniques, tricks and tactics which are proven and work, and everything is written in an easy pick-up-and-put-down format, with examples, simple illustrations and light-hearted exercises.

The intention of this book is to teach you how to become a PRO-CLO (a professional sales closer), an honest, caring and very successful individual, and also to give you the means that will make you rich in both wealth and happiness.

The contents of these pages include many lessons, examples and closes that can easily be adapted to fit any sales situation, anywhere, and to anyone. In Part One you will be taken on a staircase of thirty-nine steps, starting with sure-fire techniques and preparation, leading on to the art of successful selling, and finally culminating in asking for the order. In Part Two you will learn how to deal with objections and how to overcome the forty-two most common ones there are. Part Three is an arsenal of sixty proven closes for everyday use, your ammunition for becoming a superpower. And finally in Part Four, you will discover how to get to the top and stay there.

The techniques and closes in this encyclopedia on sales have not evolved overnight, they have been accumulated over years of success and first-hand experience in sales, in business and in training salespeople. The path of proven success is always the best one to follow, and many of the techniques and closes in this book are either from a bygone age or adapted from some of the world's greatest sales trainers of today. These, together with the secrets of a pro-clo, are now combined to create a book of such magnitude that your sales figures are guaranteed to increase.

The key to learning from this book is to make it work for you. As you read through the pages you will find that it talks to you. I urge you to talk back to it, fill it full of your scribbles and use a highlighter pen to make any important pieces stand out. Make this book yours personally and it will work for you. Refer to it time and time again, and re-read it at regular intervals. Take on board the lessons and techniques and adapt them into your everyday life. If you will do as I ask, this book will indeed make you rich.

The purpose of my writing this book is my sincere desire to pass on the secret techniques of the pro-clo. In my selling career I have personally closed in excess of £20 million of sales one on one, and I have trained thousands of salespeople from all over the world. My reason for telling you this is not to blow my own horn, but to convince you as best as I can that the techniques and closes in this book have been tried and tested and proven to work. From my experience, the most sought-after information by salespeople everywhere is information on closing the sale, and that is exactly what this book provides. It is unique because it concentrates on closing, not just on selling.

And finally, before diving in, I would like to explain that for simplicity and ease of reading I have restricted myself to the use of 'he' or 'him' rather than using literally hundreds of times 'he/she' or 'him/her'. The use of the masculine pronoun is simply for convenience, and is in no way meant to be derogative or chauvinistic. Also for ease of reading, I refer to 'a product' rather than continuously writing 'product, goods, or services'. And one last thing . . . As this is a positive book, I have assumed in the many examples that a sale will be made and therefore the purchaser will become a customer. There are many different names for a customer – a prospect, a client, an up, a lead, a buyer, a purchaser, a consumer, and so on. I prefer the name 'customer' because (a) it assumes a sale will be made and (b) it suggests that regular sales will be made.

There are no ifs, buts, or maybes about it, the techniques and closes in this book will, if you apply them, take you to the top, the best of the best, a true pro-clo.

Now it's time to go to it and begin your climb of the
thirty-nine steps to success. Good luck.

Ian Seymour

PS   The first thing you should do with this book is stick
your name on it.

PART ONE

The Thirty-Nine Steps to Success

Step I
Persistence conquers resistance

As we take this first step together, I'd like to share with you the very first rule of closing – persistence conquers resistance.

From an early age, children learn that if they persist and keep asking, they can and will overcome the resistance of parents. They learn that 'no' doesn't really mean 'NO', it simply means that they haven't convinced Mum and Dad enough yet. So they continue to put forward their case, they persist in asking until they get whatever it is they want.

This same principle applies in selling. If a pro-clo believes that his product or service will be beneficial to his customer, then he will persist until his customer is also convinced. Very often a customer will say no, but a pro-clo doesn't give up. Even when the going gets really tough, he will continue because he knows that eventually persistence will always conquer resistance and in the end both the pro-clo and the customer will benefit.

This profession called selling can be the best-paid, hardest job in the world or the worst-paid, easiest job in the world. The rewards are down to an individual's ability and effort, and only the strongest survive. The profession of selling, of closing sales, has made more millionaires than any other. A pro-clo can make more money than the company chairman who runs the company, or more money than the prime minister who runs the country, simply because in the profession of selling there is no ceiling on what you can earn. What's more, apart from achieving financial security, once you have proven yourself, once you become a pro-clo, you can benefit from working what I call 'Martini Time' – any time, any place, anywhere – and for anyone, because your skills will always be in demand.

Professional closers have attributes such as enthusiasm, confidence, a positive mental attitude, and an appetite for success. Above all, they have continuity and persistence.

Calvin Coolidge wrote:

Nothing in the world can take the place of persist-ence. Talent will not – nothing is more common than unsuccessful men with talent. Genius will not – unrewarded genius is almost a proverb. Education will not – the world is full of educated failures. Persistence and determination alone are omniportant.

Remember, the brightest lights are always the first to fade. Don't be a one-day wonder. Be consistent by being persistent.

Step 2

Positive mental attitude (PMA)

Having looked at the importance of persistence, we will now look at another, equally important, attribute of the pro-clo: a positive mental attitude (PMA).

Attitude comes from the heart and ends up in the mind.

In other words, you must first have a burning desire or need to succeed before your mind will give you the positive attitude needed to accomplish the task and continue to do so.

I am now going to show you how, with a certain attitude, you will succeed 100 per cent of the time. That's right, succeed 100 per cent of the time, with every customer you meet. Here's how. If you have the attitude that you will fail with every customer you meet, I guarantee you will be right. You *will* succeed 100 per cent of the time. You will, in fact, fail with every customer and never make a sale.

Attitude is all about belief – faith in yourself, and your ability to succeed. It has been said that only the persuaded are able to persuade. The best way to illustrate this is by way of examples. Here's an old favourite.

> Thomas Edison was the inventor of the electric light bulb. Throughout the course of his experiments, try as he might, Edison couldn't manage to make the filament last more than a few seconds. Eventually, after many hundreds of experiments, Edison was asked why he continued to persevere after failing so many times. Edison replied: 'I don't consider that I have failed hundreds of times, I have in fact succeeded in finding hundreds of ways it won't work.' After many more hundreds of experiments, Edison finally succeeded in inventing a light bulb where the filament lasted months and months and months. What persistence, what a great attitude and what a passion for success!

One of the most positive people I know and also a very good friend of mine, Luis Gonzalez, says:

The only difference between a loser and a winner is

one of attitude. The loser's attitude is, he never was, isn't now, and never will be. The winner's attitude is, he has been, still is, and will continue to be.

I remember when I was a sales manager having a problem with a salesman called Adam. Now Adam had ability, he had proven himself in the past and was a likeable chap, but over the previous couple of months he had gone straight downhill.

I tried everything to lift him up again. I went over his presentation with a fine tooth comb. I gave him incentives until they were coming out of his ears. I tried to motivate him and teach him some new tricks. I even pushed some exceptionally good leads his way in the hope that a sale would fix everything. Nothing worked, so eventually, as a last straw, I put Adam on notice. I gave him a final target: 'Three sales out of the next ten leads, otherwise you're out.'

Adam didn't want to be sacked, and I didn't want to let him go – as I said, he was a likeable chap. This is what happened.

I gave Adam the afternoon off, on condition that he would do what I was about to ask him to do, no matter how silly it might seem. After all, there is no harm in trying. Then I said to him:

'Adam, I'm going to give you the afternoon off so you can go home. Whilst you're going home, I want you to say to yourself, time and time again, "I'm going to get a deal tomorrow". Then when you get home, instead of doing whatever it is that you normally do, go into the garden, relax, and say to yourself over and over again, "I'm going to get a deal tomorrow, I'm going to get a deal tomorrow . . ." All through your shower and evening meal, drum it into yourself, "I'm going to get a deal tomorrow, I'm going to . . ." Instead of watching television, go for a long walk and repeat that statement to yourself thousands upon thousands of times until you're almost brainwashed.

'Go to bed early, and instead of reading or counting sheep, say to yourself, "I'm going to get a deal tomorrow . . ." Keep saying it until you drop asleep, and if possible, say it in your sleep. In the morning, as you get up, dressed and breakfasted, say to yourself over and over "I'm going to get a deal today". And say it all the way to work: "I'm going to get a deal today" – say it with emotion and conviction.'

Adam did as I asked and repeated that statement literally thousands of times. In doing so he embedded the statement in his subconscious, where it started to become a belief.

He doubted at first whether this advice would work and as he took his first appointment, his customer came up with a few negatives and minor objections. Adam wasn't in the slightest surprised – his doubts were confirmed. It wasn't going to work.

Then a strange phenomenon occurred. As well as negative points, the customer came up with a few positive points and buying signals. Adam's subconscious mind jumped into action as if someone had kicked him, and his subconscious said: 'Adam, hang on a minute, maybe you will get a deal today after all.' For the first time in over two months, Adam started looking for and listening to the positives. Needless to say, he made the sale and made his target, and today he is back on top again.

In the above exercise, Adam changed his attitude from negative to positive by persistently creating a desired thought-pattern. There have been many books on this subject, but for my reckoning the best is *The Power of*

Positive Thinking by Norman Vincent Peale. You would be well-advised to get yourself a copy.

If you don't have a PMA (positive mental attitude) when you meet your customer, then you're DOA (dead on arrival). PMA creates persistence and enthusiasm and success.

Step 3
Enthusiasm – to be or not to be

The only thing as contagious as enthusiasm is fear.

Later on, in Part Three (Close 5), we shall be looking at how, if it's necessary, a pro-clo will instil fear into his customer to help close the sale. For now, though, we will look at what is, without question, the most important ingredient of any sale: enthusiasm. Whether it's a market trader selling bric-a-brac, a sales rep servicing a regular account, a shop assistant selling clothes, or a commission only direct salesperson, enthusiasm creates sales.

I have read that experience and enthusiasm are rarely found together in any one individual, which gives weight to the saying 'Familiarity breeds contempt'. Let's think about that for a moment.

Picture the new recruit, fresh out of training, wet behind the ears but eager and raring to go. His product knowledge is almost non-existent and his experience *is* non-existent, but blow me down if that guy doesn't go out there and get sale after sale after sale. His enthusiasm sells to his customer because enthusiasm is contagious.

After a while, (about three months), the new re-cruit becomes the old hand. He is learning more and more and has become more experienced. He now knows his product knowledge inside out, he is confident, he is knowledgeable and well-versed. The excitement of the new challenge begins to dwindle, the element of surprise disappears with expectancy, the flame of enthusiasm flickers on the verge of becom-ing extinguished. The new hotshot recruit becomes a regular, run-of-the-mill, mediocre salesman. Another one for the pile.

This is an all too familiar story, isn't it?

It's been said that enthusiasm accounts for as much as 95 per cent of the sale, and product knowledge only 5 per cent. When you consider that a new recruit can sell and sell without knowing any closes, and only the very basic product knowledge, you appreciate just how important enthusiasm is!

Contrary to popular belief, it is possible to teach some-one how to be enthusiastic. You see, a pro-clo is one of those rare individuals who has the experience and is also able to retain enthusiasm.

Here's how. It all stems from the fact that a pro-clo is sold himself. That is to say, that he is sold on his product. So much so that when he sells to his customer he sells with enthusiasm, from the heart, not from the mouth. So the way to obtain and then retain enthusiasm is to *sell yourself first*. Once a pro-clo is sold, I mean really sold, he develops an almost fanatical belief in his product and then woe betide anybody who doesn't feel the same way.

Again, only the persuaded are able to persuade.

Remember: enthusiasm is contagious, so sell with enthusiasm, from the heart, and let it rub off on to your customers.

Step 4
Attributes of a professional closer
(pro-clo)

Professional closers have certain attributes that set them apart from everyday salesmen. Most salesmen look the part and are professional in behaviour and appearance and, like the pro-clo, they are punctual, well-groomed, courteous, reliable, smart and well-dressed. But I'm not talking about professional appearance or behaviour here. I'm talking about something deeper, I'm talking about the 'force from within' that makes the pro-clo shine and out-perform the rest. That inner confidence and absolute belief in himself. Here, then, are the attributes that make the pro-clo the best of the best, an absolute out-and-out winner.

1   A pro-clo is ambitious for success. He has an insatiable hunger, a burning desire to achieve and to succeed.

2   A pro-clo is always in command of the situation, and always aware of what is happening around him. He is able to think on his feet and he demonstrates a lot of ingenuity when faced with an unexpected problem. A pro-clo is streetwise and shrewd. He is also honest and reliable, and always delivers what he promises.

3   A pro-clo is an excellent listener and a convincing persuader. He has an acute perception and

instinctively knows what to do next. He is a natural leader – people listen to him, respect him and warm to him.

4   A pro-clo enjoys his own company as much as he enjoys others', and he often works alone because he prefers it that way. After saying that, he is always there to help out his colleagues and train the new recruits, because a pro-clo loves what he does, he gets a real buzz from his work.

5   A pro-clo abounds with enthusiasm, he has masses of initiative and energy and he gives each call 100 per cent effort. A pro-clo is the guy who, after a long and difficult sale, when he is mentally sapped and drained of energy, is still somehow able to tap into his reserves and make that last call, when anyone else would have packed up and gone home.

6   A pro-clo never seems to get sick, and even when he feels under the weather he still turns in for work. He is eager and has a great attitude.

7   A pro-clo is well-organized, he is possessive about his tools and equipment, he is meticulous in his preparations, his records are bang up-to-date and he is forever updating his figures. A pro-clo always knows where he is at.

8   A pro-clo has an air of authority about him that radiates confidence to his potential customers – he becomes their shepherd and they his flock.

9   A pro-clo is a masterful actor who is superb at creating emotion and at expressing himself. He is

also an artist who paints pictures that are so life-like they become real.

10   A pro-clo never knocks the competition. He isn't in the slightest afraid of it, instead he welcomes competition, he enjoys the challenge. A pro-clo is 100 per cent sold, right down the line. In reality, if he thought the competition was better, that's where he would be working.

11   A pro-clo is always learning new material, he is always trying to better himself and is constantly striving forward, towards his goals. He is a winner who constantly says to himself: I can, I will, I am.

12   A pro-clo motivates himself. He is a go-getter, with determination, drive and a burning passion for success. When he pumps himself up, ready for action, he radiates a glow, a force from within that creates a gut feeling, a surge of power in the pit of his belly that causes butterflies to flutter, sends tingles up his spine and puts goose bumps on his arms. Because he's invincible, he's going to win – he knows it and he feels it, from the inside out!

Recap

So far we have looked at the importance of having persistence, a positive attitude, enthusiasm, and some of the many attributes of a pro-clo. Before we move on to find out exactly how a pro-clo sells his product and closes the sale, here are a few reminders.

Step 1 Persistence always conquers resistance, eventually.

Step 2 Without a PMA (positive mental attitude) you will always be DOA (dead on arrival).

Step 3 Enthusiasm comes from the heart and it's highly contagious. Enthusiasm sells.

Step 4 Take on board the attributes of a pro-clo.

Step 5
Find a want or need

When I was a 15-year-old schoolboy, I had a Saturday job working for a local businessman, David Wood, who owned a milk round and a small chain of greengrocer shops.

One Saturday morning David gave me a box of oranges and asked me to go outside the shop and build two pyramids of oranges, one each side of the window. After completing the task, I was then asked to display price stickers by each stack of oranges. One price tag said 8 pence each, the other 12 pence each. I immediately said this couldn't be right – as all the oranges were from the same box, they couldn't be different prices! In reply I was told: 'There is always more than one market for the same product.'

It was then that I first realized that customers don't necessarily choose the cheapest options (more of this in Step 6), and that a little daring can often pay big dividends. Here was a single product displayed in two stacks within a few feet of each other for different prices, and some people actually purchased the more expensive of the two! Why? The answer is, people see what they want to see. Some customers saw the 8-pence oranges as a better buy, because you got three oranges for the price of two of the more expensive ones. Other customers perceived the 12-pence oranges as the best buy because they must have been fresher and sweeter and they would probably last longer.

The moral of this little story is, you must learn to flow with the tide and give the customer what *he* wants. Ask your customer what he finds the most attractive, the most important, the most appealing, the most beneficial, and so on, and when he tells you, give it to him with both barrels.

Note
Although, on the face of it, selling a product to different customers for different prices isn't fair, this practice has been in existence since the year dot. One of the first rules of commerce is, wherever possible, cut your costs and increase your profits. That's one of the reasons why David is such a successful businessman.

Step 6
Price

Many salespeople believe that they lose sales because of price. But in reality, most of the time, it is not the price of a product that loses a sale but the salesperson's fear of the price.

Remember, the only thing as contagious as enthusiasm is fear. If a salesperson is apprehensive about discussing price, or if a salesperson fears that a customer will say 'It costs too much', then that fear will rub off on to the customer, because fear *is* contagious.

A pro-clo understands that price will only be a problem when the customer feels that the product or service is not worth the risk, the asking price. In a nutshell, price is only a problem when someone doesn't want something badly enough. You have to create that want, you have to build value into your product so that the customer is willing to pay the price to buy it.

In the initial stages of any sale, the customer's fear of losing will be greater than his expectation of gaining. In other words, the customer will be more frightened about spending or losing his money than he will be excited about owning the product and benefiting from it. The pro-clo throughout his entire presentation builds value into his product by demonstrating how his product will satisfy the customer's needs and how the customer will benefit from owning. So at the end of the presentation, when it's time to talk money, the customer's fear of losing will no longer be greater than his expectation of gaining. In fact the complete opposite will occur. This is building value.

In his book *Supercharge Your Selling*, Nigel Henzell-Thomas suggests:

> When a prospect or customer says you're too expensive, ask whether he wants the cheapest solution or the best value for money.

I have found that they always opt for the best value for money. A pro-clo simply outweighs price with benefits and gives the customer what he perceives is the best value for money.

Understand one more thing: it is never the price that

stops people from buying (if they are sold), it's always the terms of purchase.

Let me explain: few people can afford to buy the house of their dreams for cash. What they afford is the mortgage, the terms of purchase. When the price is £100,000 the customers can't afford it (cash), but when the mortgage works out at £500 a month they can. However, they will only buy the house if they are sold on it and if paying £500 a month is worth owning it.

If you build value into your product and you have the facility to negotiate terms of purchase, price will never be a problem.

But there are some customers who, even when sold, will still tell you that it's expensive or it costs too much – these customers want to buy but are trying to see if your price is flexible first. If price starts to become an issue, try hitting it on the head with this old favourite, which is best used when it is read aloud, so have it typed on to a piece of card. (Incidentally, this quotation is well over a hundred years old.)

> It's not wise to pay too much but it's worse to pay too little. When you pay too much, you lose a little money, but that's all. When you pay too little, you sometimes lose everything, because the thing you bought was incapable of doing the thing it was bought to do.
>
> The common law of business prohibits you from paying a little and receiving a lot – it can't be done. If you deal with the lowest bidder it would be as well to add something for the risk you run and if you can do that then you can afford to pay for something better.
>
> *(John Ruskin, 1819–1900)*

Remember: if you build value into your product and

you have the facility to negotiate terms of purchase, price will never be a problem.

Step 7
Taking control

A pro-clo takes control of his customers and he leads them. It is almost as if the pro-clo were the Pied Piper with the magic flute – wherever he goes, his customers follow. He simply leads them into making the only decision possible: the decision to buy.

After all my years in the selling profession, it still never ceases to amaze me just how much a pro-clo can take command and control of another person. Customers become like putty in his hands. He is able to warm them up and mould them towards the right decision.

The customer, be it Joe Bloggs, a top executive, a company chairman, a powerful politician, or a multi-millionaire, will do exactly what the pro-clo commands, within reason. When a pro-clo says sit, stand, look at that, feel this, follow me, the customer does what he is told. This control is fantastic and the beauty of it is, the pro-clo is so natural that the customer is completely oblivious to what is happening.

This control, this air of confidence, this taking command of the situation or taking the initiative, is part of what makes a pro-clo what he is. The professional closer is not only in control of the sales situation, he is in control of his life.

So how, then, can somebody learn to take control? The answer is, *by having confidence*. If you will learn this material, highlight the important passages and read them regularly – in other words, if you practise – you will become more conversant and competent. Then you will automatically be in control, because you will have confidence.

A good tip to control a customer's attention throughout a presentation or demonstration is to use a pointer or a pen to emphasize specific features or to point out various things. To illustrate, try this little exercise and see how easy it is to control somebody else's attention.

Tell somebody (not a customer) that you are about to point to something really interesting and exciting with your pen. Ask him to deliberately concentrate on not looking. Then point to something, tap it with your pen and say: 'Just look at that.' He will do – and when he does, move your pen and point to something else, tap it and say: 'Look at that and that and that.'

That's what I call taking control. In the above exercise we are obviously abusing that control to demonstrate a point, but in real-life selling the control is so discreet that the customer is not aware of what is happening. And a pro-clo would never do anything to abuse a customer.

Step 8
Prejudging

This next step relates to a qualified prospect. For example, someone who has answered an advert, responded to a marketing campaign, looked at the competition, or walked into your shop, office, or showroom with a genuine interest. It does not relate to unqualified prospects or leads, which we will look at in Step 13.

The saying 'You can't judge a book by its cover' is never truer than in the sales industry. Regardless of where people live, what colour they are, how old or how young someone is, what a person does for a living, what religion or sex they are; regardless of appearance or dress, and regardless of whatever excuse or objection is voiced, nobody, and I mean no single person, is able to determine beforehand which prospects are buyers and which are not. If it were possible for a person to determine which prospective customers were going to buy, there would be no such thing as a pro-clo, simply because there would be no need for them.

At the end of the day, no salesperson alive can tell (and be 100 per cent sure) whether or not he has a sale until the money is on the table. To prejudge that customers aren't going to buy before giving a full presentation is suicide. If your product were free, everyone would have one, wouldn't they? Therefore, the only thing that stops people from buying is money, and until you look at the figures, until the price is on the table, you can never tell. For that reason the pro-clo always gives it his best shot, he gives 100 per cent effort to each customer, and his sales figures speak for themselves.

The pro-clo knows that every customer or prospect he sees has been sold to before by someone. All he has to do is be as good as, or better than, that someone. The pro-clo also emphatically believes that each qualified client he sees should buy his product. The reason for this belief is that every pro-clo is completely sold himself.

Once again . . . only the persuaded are able to persuade.

For my money, there isn't a salesperson anywhere who hasn't experienced the situation where he thought there was no chance of a sale, then lo and behold, from nowhere the client became a customer.

One more time – if you have a qualified client or customer, never assume that they're not going to buy.

Let's now look at an example of a salesperson prejudging his potential customers.

> Supposing a couple respond to a marketing campaign from a timeshare company and they go along to have a look. After a while the salesperson, who has now prejudged the couple, says: 'I can't sell to this couple. He's 45, she's 20 and a different colour, they're not married, they don't own a house and have only been in their rented accommodation for four months. He's a market trader with no accountant and she's unemployed with bad debts, and to top it all off, they've seen the competition and didn't buy because they couldn't afford it. I just haven't got a chance with these people!'

If you look for negatives, guess what you find? Obviously the above example is an extreme one, but let's now look at how a pro-clo would handle the same situation.

> First of all, the pro-clo listens to the information from his customers but what he hears is not negative, it's positive. He knows that his customers have an interest in his product because they have responded to an advert or marketing campaign.
>
> Second, the pro-clo knows that a market trader with no accountant deals in cash and quite possibly has black money (undeclared earnings/cash from under the table).
>
> Third, the pro-clo knows that if his customers have seen the competition and didn't buy, it was probably

because the competition prejudged the customers and
didn't allow them the opportunity to buy. Instead of
treating the customers like time-wasters, or outcasts,
the pro-clo treats them like a King and Queen.

Finally, the pro-clo knows that where there is a
will there is a way and with his special kind of
treatment, he will find that way. After all, who is
to say that the customers don't have a nice little
nest egg tucked away somewhere? Until the price is
on the table, you never know!

We have said before that customers come in all different
shapes, sizes, ages, colours, creeds, and so on, but all
human beings have certain characteristics in common. All
our desires, needs and wants are very similar, and as
human beings we all have the same senses and the same
emotions and we all think very similarly. Zig Ziglar, in
his excellent book *Zig Ziglar's Secrets of Closing the Sale*,
demonstrates this point superbly. The following exercise
is an extract from his book, which I have added to and
adapted slightly.

To prove how similarly we all think, answer the
following questions as quickly as you can and don't
change your mind.

1 Think of a number between one and ten.
2 Think of a colour.
3 Think of a flower.
4 Using your writing hand, hold up three fingers.
5 Think of a fruit.
6 Think of a vegetable.
7 Think of an item of furniture.
8 Think of an animal.

Now let's see how your answers compare.

1   Seven.
2   Red.
3   Rose.
4   Held up all but your thumb and little finger.
5   Apple or orange.
6   Carrot.
7   Chair.
8   Dog or cat.

It doesn't matter how many answers you agreed with.
I didn't say we were all exactly alike. I said we were
all very similar.

The point I am trying to hammer home is, all your
prospects are similar too. So don't prejudge, because you
never can tell!

Recap

It's time we had a little refresher to make sure that you
remember to use each step on the staircase, so that you don't
trip and fall over.

Step 5   Find a want or need and then satisfy it.

Step 6   Using customer benefits, build value into your
         product so that price will never be a problem.

Step 7   Radiate confidence and take control.

Step 8   Never prejudge that a qualified prospect isn't going
         to buy, because then you will be right.

Step 9
Ten do's to ten don'ts

A book on Sales wouldn't be complete without some guidelines, some do's and don'ts to follow. In our industry there are literally thousands of these rules, many of them unwritten. Some are just plain common sense, and others nothing more than common decency but there are some that really do make a difference.

Ask anyone who is successful, and they will tell you that they adopt the teachings of other successful people and then adapt those teachings to their own lives. This in itself is plain common sense because the path of proven success is always the best and easiest to follow.

Here then, are some important do's and don'ts that really do make a difference. I urge you to take them on board and adapt them to your own life.

The Do's

1   *Leave your work at work.*
    Don't take work home with you. Every pro-clo needs to relax and recharge his batteries, so that he is at his best for the following day. No matter how much we enjoy our work, the rule is: 'We work to live, not live to work.' Spending quality time and relaxing with our family is the key to real happiness and prosperity. A true pro-clo knows how and when to turn off.

2   *Take regular exercise.*
    It is a well-known fact that a healthy body leads to
    a healthy mind. If you read this and say to your-
    self 'I really must do some exercise', and then end
    up doing nothing about it, you haven't got what it
    takes to be a true pro-clo. On the other hand, if you
    don't feel you should take regular exercise, I urge
    you to consider the following.
       Regular exercise increases your stamina, and
    makes you sharper and more alert. Regular ex-
    ercise makes you healthier. It makes you less prone
    to common ailments such as colds or influenza as
    well as major illnesses such as diabetes or heart
    conditions. Regular exercise makes you feel good
    about yourself. It makes you feel fit and alive and it
    keeps you younger than your years. Regular exercise
    increases your metabolism, which burns up calories
    and thus keeps your weight down. Most important
    of all, regular exercise increases your chances of a
    longer, healthier life which means you will have more
    time to enjoy your blessings and your spoils.
       I'm not saying you should become a health freak or
    a fanatical athlete, but a *minimum* exercise programme
    should be 30+ minutes three times a week. Obviously,
    if you have any doubts about taking exercise, you
    should seek medical advice first. The rule is, don't
    not do it, just don't overdo it.

3   *Create a list of things to do.*
    In order of importance, and as you complete each
    task, cross that item off the list. This is an 'oldie'
    and nowadays you can even buy pads with 'Things
    To Do' pre-printed on them. When his mind is buzz-
    ing in a confused state, trying to remember all the
    things that he must do, a pro-clo doesn't get into a

flutter. He simply creates his 'Things To Do' list and relieves himself from the pressure to remember. He can then concentrate on tackling his work in order of importance. In doing so the pro-clo is able to see, in black and white, just where he is going and what he has accomplished. It also gives him a great sense of achievement when he gets to cross off the last item.

4   *Do what you don't want to do.*
    If you are scared of something (maybe cold calling or a specific objection), you become insecure and lack confidence. This causes procrastination, so that you're indecisive about what you should do. Always do whatever you are scared of, whatever you dislike, whatever you fear, and you will eventually learn to overcome it because 'Familiarity breeds contempt'. There is only one sure way of never failing, and that is never to try. If you don't try, you won't lose, but you won't win either. Winners do what they fear to do.

5   *Dress like a professional.*
    Here, I am not just talking about dress in the clothes sense, but everything from personal hygiene to the wearing of jewellery, even to the condition and appearance of your sales aids. A pro-clo knows that appearance is of paramount importance to portray a confident, successful and professional image. Ask yourself, am I dressed like somebody I would want to do business with?

6   *Be courteous and smile.*
    Suffice it for me to say 'Actions speak louder than words'. Here's a little poem I wrote about being courteous, followed by another from an unknown author explaining the wonders of a smile.

COURTESY

Always be there when you say you will,
Don't move around when you should be still,
Open a door, pull out a chair,
Say please and thank you, and show that you care,
Offer help whenever you can,
Never offend a no-smoking ban,
Ask if they're comfortable, offer a drink,
Little things mean more than you think.
Do this, and respect their point of view,
And success will always come to you.

(R.I.S.)

A SMILE

A smile costs nothing, but gives you much.
It enriches those who receive,
without making poorer those who give.
It takes but a moment, but the memory of it lasts forever.
None is so rich or mighty that he can get along without it,
and none is so poor but that he can be made rich by it.
A smile creates happiness in the home,
fosters good will in business
and is the countersign of friendship.
It brings rest to the weary,
cheer to the discouraged,
sunshine to the sad
and is nature's best antidote for trouble.
Yet, it cannot be bought, begged, borrowed or stolen,
for it is something of No Value until it is Given Away.
Some people are too tired to give you a smile.
Give them one of yours, as none needs a smile so much
as he who has no more to give!

(Author unknown)

7   *Accept when you're wrong.*
When you make a mistake or you're in the wrong, don't shy away from it. Instead, accept it and learn from it. A pro-clo will always admit when he is wrong. He knows that no-one ever choked swallowing their pride.

8   *Motivate yourself.*
Each morning and before each call, motivate yourself, give yourself that edge, that buzz, that force from within that tells you you're good, you're very good. Let the confidence ooze out of every pore, let the butterflies fly in your stomach and the tingles run up your spine. The pro-clo switches himself on, he psyches himself up, and it's easy, because he instinctively knows 'he's gonna win'.

Professional closers motivate themselves, they don't need others to do it for them. They listen to great motivational music or inspirational tapes, they psych themselves up in front of a mirror, they pace up and down drumming positive thoughts into their subconscious minds and they read good motivational material, just as you are doing now with this book.

Motivation stimulates excitement and enthusiasm and the winning attitude needed to succeed.

9   *Set yourself goals.*
It is important to have something to strive for. Otherwise you end up wandering around without a destination, like a piece of driftwood on the ocean. People become stale when their goals and dreams equal their present being. They lack desire and ambition, and end up existing instead of thriving. A pro-clo sets himself goals and, as he nears or attains them, he sets himself new desires, new goals, and off he goes again,

always thriving. (This is discussed in depth in Step 39.)

10 *Give more than you need to.*
Always give the customer more than is expected, that little extra, that complimentary add-on, or going the extra mile when it comes to service. Not only does this solidify a deal, but it gives you repeat business, referral business and a reputation that will create new business.

The Don'ts

1 *Don't use red.*
Never write with a red pen, or wear a red shirt/dress/blouse when you are with a customer. Subconsciously red signifies danger, stop, beware, anger, red alert. Although these negative thoughts are not in the forefront of the customer's mind, they are nevertheless there, warning the customer to be wary.
   You wouldn't wave a red rag at a bull to win favour, so don't do it to a customer.

2 *Don't wear dark sunglasses when you are with a customer.*
This gives the impression that you have something to hide, that you are a shady character who cannot be trusted. Eye contact is a must for the pro-clo.
   By the same token, it's impossible to read a customer wearing dark glasses, and you should ask him politely to remove them. I find a little humour works best. Try saying 'Mr Jones, what colour are your eyes?' When he answers, say 'Would you mind proving it to me?' (Raise your eyebrows and give him a knowing smile.) Works every time!

3 *Don't ask certain questions.*
Never ask a customer if he understands. Not want-ing to appear stupid, he will always answer 'Yes', even when he wants to say 'No'. Never say to a customer 'You know what I mean', or 'Do you get my drift?' Again, he will always answer 'Yes' when he might mean 'No'. Instead, ask 'Are you happy with that?', 'Do you have any questions?', 'Did you follow that or shall I go over it again?'.

Also, never say to a customer 'Let me be honest' or 'To tell you the truth', because it implies that you weren't before. When someone says they'll be honest with you, it generally means the opposite!

4 *Don't knock the competition.*
This has an adverse effect. The customer will think that you are trying to hide behind the competition or that you are trying to justify an inadequacy in your product. A pro-clo doesn't knock the competition, he welcomes it, and sometimes he will even compare the competition's product with his own in front of a customer. Remember what we said earlier. The pro-clo is sold on his product 100 per cent. If he thought the competition was better, he would be working for them. It is this belief, this conviction, that makes the customer buy.

5 *Don't live in the past.*
Reminiscing can be fun and enjoyable, but only to the person doing the reminiscing. It's the 'also-rans' in life who live off past performance and an old worn-out reputation. There is nothing wrong with looking back, now and again – but remember, being in reverse won't take you forward.

6   *Don't fight change, welcome it.*
Change has always caused, and always will cause, insecurity, doubt, unfamiliarity and fear. A pro-clo knows this but he understands that change is necessary. Without it we would all still be in the Stone Age living in caves. A pro-clo knows that change is good, it keeps people on their toes, it demonstrates a will to progress and to improve. Above all else, change creates a new challenge and every pro-clo loves a good challenge. So he doesn't fight change, he encourages it.

7   *Don't stop learning.*
A pro-clo is forever reading new material, listening to cassettes and gaining new information. He is always updating his portfolio of techniques and closes and gathering new tools. A pro-clo has a relentless desire, a burning passion for improvement. He has an unquenchable thirst for knowledge and he soaks up all positive material like a sponge.

A pro-clo knows that the key to continuous success is continuous learning. If you stop learning you will eventually begin to decline. It's like travelling in a hot air balloon. To ascend to greater heights you need to continuously supply fuel. If you shut off the fuel supply (stop learning) you will hang in suspension for a while, but inevitably you will begin to descend.

I wrote this book in such a way that it is easy to pick up and put down, because I know it is impossible to absorb all the lessons in one go. I implore you again to keep reading this book at regular intervals, use it as your personal sales manual, and keep learning. Don't ever stop, don't become content with mediocrity, don't remain stationary because if you do you will start to decline. Let me put it this way:

To discover how to be a true pro-clo
Continue to learn and continue to grow.

8   *Don't waste time.*
Time is the most precious thing in the world, and life
is too short to waste it. A pro-clo makes full use of
his time, he plans how to use it to give optimum
benefit. However, things don't always go according
to plan, and when a pro-clo finds he has time on
his hands, he doesn't loaf around. Instead, he asks
himself: 'What is the most worthwhile thing I could
be doing right now?' When he comes up with the
answer, he gets straight to it!
   Remember to plan time for recreation and with your
family and don't get side-tracked. A pro-clo plans
his time and times his plan.

9   *Don't give losers the time of day.*
In every sales organization there is always a group of
negative salespeople that you should avoid like the
plague. These losers are so easy to spot – they're
the ones that take an hour over a gallon of coffee
before they start work in the morning, the ones that are
forever hanging around the office or canteen and the
ones that congregate in the pub after work to drown
their sorrows. All these losers seem to do is complain,
make up excuses, spread gossip and start rumours.
   All losers are sinking, and they are so afraid of going
under that they try to pull everyone else down with
them, thinking that they will find safety in numbers.
When all is said and done, these birds of a feather will
always flock together and there is very little you or I
can do to change that. In this instance, the old saying
'If you can't beat them, join them' is wrong. A pro-clo

says 'If you can't beat them, avoid them' – but do it politely, there is no point in adding fuel to their fire.

In staying away from the losers a pro-clo often alienates himself, but that doesn't really bother him. He knows that sometimes 'it's tough at the top', but it's always tougher at the bottom.

10 *Don't ever give up.*
Fight the good fight, and when all else fails, when you're in dire straits, when there is no hope whatsoever, admit defeat. There is no shame in it – but before you do, try another close.

DON'T QUIT
When things go wrong as they sometimes will,
When the road you're trudging seems all uphill,
When the funds are low and the debts are high,
And you want to smile but you have to sigh,
When care is pressing you down a bit,
Rest if you must, but don't you quit.
Success is failure turned inside out,
The silver tint in the clouds of doubt,
And you never can tell how close you are,
It may be near when it seems afar.
So stick to the fight when you're hardest hit,
It's when things go wrong that you mustn't quit.
(Author unknown)

Recap: Step 9

The Do's
1 Leave your work at work
2 Take regular exercise
3 Create a 'things to do' list

The Don'ts
1 Don't use red
2 Don't wear dark sunglasses
3 Don't ask certain questions

4 Do what you don't want to do	4 Don't knock the competition
5 Dress like a professional	5 Don't live in the past
6 Be courteous and smile	6 Don't fight change, welcome it
7 Accept when you're wrong	7 Don't stop learning
8 Motivate yourself	8 Don't waste time
9 Set yourself goals	9 Don't give losers the time of day
10 Give more than you need to	10 Don't ever give up

Step 10

Tips for selling on the customer's home turf

The following tips are directed at selling on the customer's homebase, that is, his house or place of work. However, as with all lessons in this book, these tips can and should be adapted to fit any sales situation, anywhere.

1 If a call of nature is imminent, relieve yourself prior to meeting your customer! Now, before you drop this book in surprise at this tip, let me explain why.

 If possible you should stick to your customers like glue, from the first moment you meet them until it's time to wave goodbye. You should marry them, stay with them and don't give them an opportunity to scheme up ways of saying no when you're not around.

2 Don't be late for an appointment, not even by a minute. A first impression is a lasting impression, so make a good start by being punctual. If you are held up, or a delay is unavoidable, always phone your

customer *before* the pre-arranged time to apologize and reschedule.

3   Never park your car in a 'reserved' space, it might belong to the MD! If you are in any doubt, ask where you can park. Alternatively park at the far end of the car park, the end that is farthest away from the building. (One of the status symbols of anybody who is anybody is that they get to park nearest the building.)

   This same principle applies at the customer's home. Appreciate that there are certain places the customer reserves for his own parking or that of his family. To avoid any possible irritation, don't park on the customer's drive, don't block the driveway and don't park in front of the window or garage. Not only is this being courteous but it means that you won't be disturbed during your presentation (or closing) when the customer's son arrives and wants to put his car away.

4   Leave all your sales equipment in the car and be empty-handed when you greet your customer. If you are carrying all your sales material, samples and equipment, apart from the fact it will be difficult to shake hands, you will appear too impersonal and too ready for action. Think how you would feel, if immediately upon opening the door of a tailor's shop, the sales assistant said hello and began measuring you with his tape.

   (Once you have greeted the customer you should then excuse yourself whilst you go and get your things.)

5   When you greet your customers, always shake hands with them – you might as well get them used to it from the start.

6   As you enter the customer's domain, make an exaggerated effort in wiping your feet. The customer will notice this mark of respect and will warm to you more easily.

7   Always ask or wait to be seated. Remember a man's home (or his office for that matter) is his castle. If you are invited into his castle you are a guest, so make sure you act like a guest, not an intruder.

8   If we invite someone round to our home, most of us make an effort to make ourselves and our home more presentable. We dust and polish and tidy round, we spray a little air freshener, put flowers into a vase and bring out the best chinaware.
    If you notice a nice, tidy, clean home, then mention it – compliment your customers sincerely and they will love you for it – because that effort was made on your behalf. Likewise you should compliment a tidy and well-organized office.

9   Don't jump in with both feet. Don't move straight into your sales presentation. Instead, settle things down and induce a receptive atmosphere. (This subject will be discussed in more detail in Step 18.)

10 If you come from a different ethnic or cultural background from your customer, always accept and consume an offer of food or drink. This will put your customer at ease and show him that you are not prejudiced.

11 Look around and you will see photographs, paintings, certificates, trophies, books, plants, record collections, cats, dogs, model planes, musical instruments . . . the

list goes on and on. These items are memorabilia or passions to your customer, so mention them. Ask and be sincerely inquisitive and your customers will love you for it. Let them go on and on about the things they have a passion for and they will feel *so* appreciative – because they're enjoying themselves and it's very rare that they get the chance to show off to a willing audience. That appreciation will turn to obligation and they will end up saying: 'Well, enough of that – show me what you've got – how much is it? OK, I'll have one.'

12 Never ignore the customer's children. Instead recruit them to your side and they'll be your biggest ally. (In an office you might not recruit the spectator but you should never ignore him.)

13 Don't invade a customer's desk with your 'things' without asking first. Likewise don't use a customer's furniture or floor (as in carpet) without asking. This is especially pertinent when it comes to glasses, cups, or plates. Many customers are too polite to ask you to move something but the offending object remains on their mind and it festers. When this happens they won't be giving you their undivided attention – so always ask first.

14 Always get the customer involved in the presentation, not just verbally but physically. Get the customer to help set up your demonstration, get him to compare colour co-ordination or help you measure up. Get the customer to look, touch, smell, taste and listen. (This subject is discussed in depth in Step 26.) The more involved he is, the more enthusiastic he becomes, because he starts to envisage what it would be like to own

your product. Take him, as it were, for a test drive and let him feel what it's really like to be behind the wheel!

15 When you are in the customer's home or office you are less in control of outside events, such as an interruption by another member of the family, a knock at the door, or a telephone call. When this happens, stop your presentation and make small talk until everyone returns – then backtrack slightly to refresh their memories.

16 It is always a good idea to leave something (of no intrinsic value) behind when you leave. For example, you could accidentally on purpose forget your folder, which must have fallen under the table, or maybe your calculator, that slipped down the side of your chair. This little trick gives you a 'legitimate' excuse to call back again tomorrow. At the same time you can consolidate the deal or sell them some more, or if you failed the first time, have another go!

Recap: Step 10

1 Stick to your customers like glue. Marry them.
2 Don't be late. If it's unavoidable, phone before your appointment time.
3 Park your car with care.
4 Leave your equipment in the car until after the greeting.
5 Shake hands – get them used to it.
6 Wipe your feet well.
7 Ask or wait to be seated.
8 Compliment a tidy abode.
9 Don't jump in with both feet.

10 Accept an offer of tea or coffee.
11 Encourage talk about passions.
12 Don't ignore the spectators.
13 Ask before you put down your things.
14 Involve your customers, physically.
15 Wait out any interruptions.
16 Leave an object so that they can't *object* to a second visit.

Step 11
A dozen little tricks of the trade

Before you jump into this 'fun' section, I would like to make one point absolutely clear. *Never burn your customers.* A pro-clo would never do anything detrimental to a customer – it's not in his nature. If you cheat, lie, misrepresent, or mislead to hurt or harm a customer for your own gain, then you are a con-man. Make no mistake about it, there is a world of difference between the 'honourable' intentions and ploys of a pro-clo and the 'dishonourable' conduct and scams of a con-man. When a pro-clo uses a little pressure or some sort of ploy, he does so because he believes it's in his customer's (and his own) best interest. On the other hand, when the con-man is in action, there is only one person's interest on *his* mind!

I can't really put my finger on it, maybe it's the 'power from above', but con-men don't seem to enjoy health, wealth, happiness, or security for very long. I hope this point sinks in: DON'T BURN THEM.

Here, then, are a dozen little tricks of the trade and how to apply them.

1   *How to stop the rot.*
If a customer loses interest, if he starts to wander or
to lean away from the table and sits back in his chair,
don't inch forward, don't climb up on to the table and
push your material under his nose. If you do he will
back off even farther. Instead, copy him. That's right,
copy him! Sit way back in your chair and continue
talking . . . but *so* quietly that it's impossible for the
customer to hear you . . . the customer will instinctively
come forward, back into position again.

If it happens a second time, then lower your voice, pull
your material towards you and, pointing to something,
enthusiastically say to the customer: 'Just read that.'
This will bring the customer back into action again.

If it should happen a third time, stop in your tracks,
become concerned and say to the customer: 'Was I
talking too loudly for you?' The customer will become uncomfortable and deny it, but from now on
he will pay a lot more attention.

2   *Taking immediate control.*
Always move your customer as soon as possible after
the preliminary greeting. This technique puts the pro-
clo in charge immediately because it allows *him* to
choose the turf, rather than the customer. This changing
of positions makes the customer somewhat disorien-
tated and submissive, which automatically puts the
instigator, the pro-clo, in control.

Changing the position or the turf must be done
in an affable manner and there are various ways of
accomplishing this. For example, changing rooms for
more peace and quiet, changing chairs because this
one is more comfortable, or changing to a different
position for more light, heat, breeze, and so on. If
you are in the customer's home or office you might

suggest that you move from the lounge to the kitchen table. Or ask if the customer wouldn't mind sitting here instead of there, as you are slightly deaf in one ear and are finding it difficult to hear him. Just how or where you move your customer isn't important, as long as he moves from where he chooses to be to where you choose him to be.

3   *One way to overcome procrastination.*
I once heard of a salesman who used melodramatics to overcome customer procrastination. He would set the alarm on his watch to go off ten minutes after he met his customers. When the alarm activated, he would apologize and explain to his customers that it was imperative that he take his tablets. He would even request a glass of water. He then went on to explain that he suffered from a serious complaint and that the pills (vitamin tablets in an old prescription bottle) stopped him from becoming overstressed or excited and allowed him to lead as normal a life as possible.

Of course, throughout the presentation, the salesman's 'illness' was completely forgotten, and it was never mentioned again unless the customers began to procrastinate. The salesman would be enthusiastic and excited when attempting to actually close the sale, and if he ever encountered any real indecisiveness, he would stop suddenly, frown and tap his chest once or twice, then continue as if nothing had happened. Apparently, his customers always decided very quickly after that!

This salesman's antics may be controversial and I don't wholly recommend them, but I was told that his intentions were always honourable and he always got more referrals than any of his colleagues.

4   *An 'oldie' to create urgency.*
Although this one has been over-used across the years, and many customers are now sceptical, the impending price increase can still be very effective in creating urgency. Here is an example which demonstrates just how effective this closing tool can be.

My neighbour recently purchased some replacement windows. He had originally intended to shop around and compare prices but he ended up buying on the first quote. Afterwards he explained to me that the reason he had been so impulsive was because he was getting such a good deal. Amongst other things the salesperson had produced a price list, dated two days before, showing a 10 per cent increase in prices with immediate effect. The salesperson offered to backdate my neighbour's quote by three days if he decided there and then to go ahead.

My neighbour is now the proud owner of some beautiful double-glazed windows, a new front door and new patio doors!

5   *Customer guidance from above.*
When it's time to close, if possible, sit higher than the customer so that they have to look up to you. (Use a different chair or a cushion or simply straighten your posture.) By sitting slightly higher than the customer you become dominant – the customer looks up to you, he respects your knowledge and becomes a little submissive, he looks to you for reassurance and guidance. From this position the pro-clo simply guides him home. (This is the same reason why a bank manager or a sales manager's chair is often higher than the other chairs in the office – so they can dominate their captives.)

6   *The deliberate mistake.*
     A beautiful little ploy to test the water, to find out
     how the customer feels about the product and to
     see if he is thinking ownership thoughts yet, is to
     use a deliberate mistake. For example, the customer
     has said earlier that he didn't like the large one, it
     was too bulky. When the pro-clo feels the time is
     right, he makes a deliberate mistake to see if his
     customer corrects him. For example:

     PRO-CLO: 'I personally prefer the smaller unit, but
     you said earlier that you thought the larger one would
     best suit your needs.'
     CUSTOMER: 'No, I said the larger one was too
     bulky.'
     PRO-CLO: 'Oh, I'm sorry – so it's the smaller unit
     you'd like to have?'

     If the customer says 'yes', get out the order form and
     start writing it up. If the customer says 'I haven't
     decided anything yet', you carry on from where you
     left off.

7   *Trick or treat with the wrong price.*
     Here's another adaptation of the deliberate mistake.
     This one is best used with the pushy customer.
         Give the customer the correct price, then after a
     minute or two, apologize and tell the customer you've
     made a mistake, you've used an old price list. The
     prices have gone up since then and now it should
     be £+++. The customer will object and say 'I'm not
     paying that for it . . . You made the mistake, I want
     it for the old price.' (I think your sales manager might
     just give in!) Be very careful with this one, you don't
     want the customer to think you're incompetent, or
     that you're trying to pull the wool over his eyes.

8   *Make a spectacle of yourself when you mean
business.*
This technique belongs to a very successful closer
and an old colleague, Barbara.

Now Barbara is the sort of salesperson who really
befriends her customers, she has a great personality
and she gets very close to the people she is selling to.
However, this presents Barbara with a rather unique
problem. You see she gets so close to her customers,
that it can be, and very often is, difficult to get
down to business, without being rude or abrupt. To
overcome this dilemma, Barbara doesn't say a thing,
she simply takes out a pair of spectacles and puts
them on. Her customers immediately feel the tactful
change and respond accordingly.

This 'putting on the spectacles' trick works every
time because it forces the customer to look at things
in a different perspective.

9   *Win the wife and you'll win the husband.*
If your customers are a married couple, concentrate
the most effort in selling to the wife, because 99 per
cent of the time if she's sold the husband will follow
suit.

Most men follow their wives' decisions and they
will do almost anything to please them, so win the
wife and you'll win the husband.

10 *An ace up your sleeve called obligation.*
Giving the occasional gift is a gesture which often
produces excellent results. This practice is sometimes
known as gifting, and the art of making it work
is to offer a plausible explanation of why you are
giving the gift. Every customer knows that 'There is
no such thing as a free lunch', so don't be obvious

about it. The customer should never feel you are trying to bribe him or buy his business. Generally speaking, the gift should be inexpensive, and if possible it should be a personal gift – it is not the cost but the thought that counts. For example, the gift could be a box of cigars which were given to you for Christmas (but you don't smoke cigars); two tickets for the match on Saturday (you've now got to go to a wedding); a case of wine that a customer gave to you (you're tee-total but didn't have the heart to tell him); or even a couple of T-shirts with your company logo on them, for his kids.

Some of the big companies really go to town when it comes to gifting established accounts and would-be customers. Crates of booze at Christmas, private boxes at the races, conferences and dinners at the best hotels, and so on. They don't call it gifting, they call it expenses or perks that go on their entertainment allowance. But in reality it's 'speculate to accumulate', and the companies recoup these expenses many times over.

Gifting creates gratitude, but when it's time to close that gratitude turns into obligation. A pro-clo firmly believes that every penny spent on a customer is worth a pound, so don't be afraid of putting your hand in your pocket.

11 *The best little ringer in town.*
The telephone is one of the best closing tools around, and more sales have been closed through pretend telephone conversations than through bona fide calls. A telephone can be used quite genuinely to check inventory, receive authorization, check delivery schedules and so on – and when the need arises, a little invented call can work wonders at creating urgency.

Here are a few examples.

'Is it still available?'

'What do we have left, if anything, in this range?'

'What do you mean, it's sold? When? Is the other one still there?'

'So you would need to know now for delivery next Thursday?'

'Could we possibly see our way to allow them . . . ?'

'OK, I understand the answer is no . . . but what if . . .?'

'By the way, can you send six more to Johnson's for tomorrow morning?'

'Listen, Jim, I was wondering if I could call in that favour . . .'

12 *The deal of the decade.*

The 'golden oldie' is to build the extra discount into your price, so that you can offer added incentives and entice the customer to buy without deviating from the original price, or making a loss. A gentleman I know (now a multi-millionaire) used to own a second-hand car lot. In his younger days, his customers would snap his hands off because he would offer up to £1,000 more on the trade-in value of their old car. (He simply used to add £1,000 on to his asking price.)

The reason he is now a millionaire is because he always gave the customer the extra £1,000 trade-in value, even when he knew he didn't have to. As a result, Jack always had more referrals than all the local competition put together.

If the cause is just, a pro-clo is definitely not faint-hearted about using ploys or pressure to convince his

customers of the right decision – but he never pushes
his customers, he pulls them.

Before reaching this section, I have already shared
with you some of the many tips, tricks and tactical
moves of the pro-clo, and throughout the remainder of
the book you will find literally hundreds more. However,
before we move on I would like to reiterate my opening
remarks to this section. Never burn your customers and
never do anything detrimental to a customer.

Step 12

Do your homework

As we continue our climb up 'The Thirty-Nine Steps to
Success' we shall look in depth at how a pro-clo actually
sells to his customers. Now we are going to look at how
he prepares for the encounter.

Nowadays, especially in direct selling, many companies
provide their salespeople with qualified leads obtained
through various advertising and marketing campaigns. In
such situations a great deal of homework can be done
before the pro-clo even meets the customer. Apart from
the obvious qualifications and information that the customers give the marketing department, there are a number
of other telltale signs that the pro-clo searches for and
picks up on. We will look at some examples of this in a
moment.

A pro-clo always does his homework before making a
presentation. Even on a cold call, he doesn't just knock
on doors for the sake of knocking on doors – he does his
research and knocks on the right doors. Depending upon

the product or service, this homework or groundwork can be very comprehensive and time-consuming, but it is work that must be done. A pro-clo finds out as much as possible about his potential customer, he finds out about his lifestyle, his family, his concerns, interests, hobbies, wants, needs, aspirations, likes, dislikes and whatever else he can find out that is pertinent. Armed with this ammunition, the pro-clo is able to locate the customer's hot-button, the thing that is going to switch him on. When he moves into his presentation the pro-clo (because he has done his homework) shows the customer that he has a problem, an itch, a want, a need, a hurt, and then offers the customer a solution, a medicine that will cure everything. When a pro-clo does his homework effectively, the customer is so relieved to be offered a solution that he doesn't need to be closed, he eagerly buys without any hesitation. These are the best kind of sales, the ones that lie down and roll over for you. They are also the kind of sales that provide excellent testimonials and great referrals.

Here, then, are a few of the telltale signs that a pro-clo will pick up on when he is doing his homework. (Although a pro-clo picks up on this information, he does not prejudge – he is simply aware. Forewarned is forearmed.) Let's take the customer's name, address and telephone number as a typical example of how seemingly trivial information can provide the pro-clo with crucial clues about his customer, without ever having met him.

Forenames can give you a clue to age . . . If the customer's forenames are Arthur, Harold, Percival, Wilbur, or Alice, Edith, Gladys, Lilian, etc., the chances are, with these types of old-fashioned name, they are getting on in years. (I know that old-fashioned names have, over recent years, become fashionable

again, but it is unlikely that today's youth are going
to be potential customers for at least another 15–20
years.)

Surnames can reveal things about class and attitude
. . . If the customer has a double-barrel surname, e.g.
Foster-Smith, or Freedman-Jones, it might suggest
that the customer is a little flamboyant or loud, it
could be that he wants to be noticed and stand
out from the crowd. These types of customer have
a big ego. (Take them on a trip.) The same normally
applies to a customer who offers his/her middle name
or initial without being asked for it.

Titles and marital status . . . Look carefully at what
information titles reveal about marital status. For
instance, if a couple have two surnames and, say,
a Mr Smith is living with a Miss Jones, they are
obviously not married, probably don't have children,
and may have two incomes. If, on the other hand,
Mr Smith is living with a Mrs Jones, she at least
will have been married and there may be more than
one set of children. They could be living together
and not divorced, so money might be tight and offering finance could be a problem.

An address can tell you a lot about a prospective
customer . . . If someone gives a house name in their
address, such as Beavers Lodge or Rose Cottage, etc.,
then they are more often than not very houseproud
and have a lovely home. They also like to flaunt
it.
   If the house number is very high, e.g. No. 363 or
No. 1247, it normally indicates that the people live
in a block of flats, a very large busy road, or on a

massive estate. Such people tend to be honest and hard-working, they tend to be very down-to-earth, and are not frightened to spend money. That's why they are now a lead.

If the address reads Something Road, or Something Street, then the property is usually quite old and normally a terrace, which means it will probably have two or three bedrooms. A little research of the area will give you an idea of property values, so you can get a general idea of their likely income and outgoings.

If the address reads No. 3 The Dingle, or Bluebell Close, Bearswood – or how about Avenue, Lane, etc. – this gives the impression of a rather big house in a nice area.

Also pay attention to telephone numbers . . . If a customer gives his telephone number as Bearswood 1234 instead of giving his area code, he's being snobbish, he wants to let people know he lives in an affluent area. Easy to sell to!

This is straightforward stuff, yet the average salesperson doesn't see it and doesn't think to look. Of course, this is only the tip of the iceberg and a pro-clo would gather much more information than name, address and phone number – but the above examples will give you a feel for what I am trying to get across.

Doing your homework is a very necessary step on the staircase and if you try to jump over it, you will almost certainly fall down. It is also, very often, a painful step, but as the saying goes: 'If there is no pain there's no gain.' Remember a pro-clo is AWARE – forewarned *is* forearmed.

Step 13
Canvassing for business

Some pro-clos benefit from quality leads through their
company marketing departments, some do not. Whichever
is the case, a pro-clo is always on the hunt for leads which
could generate new business. Here are some ideas that I
have always found rewarding.

Hit 'em again, Sam
The best source of new business is repeat business from
existing customers, so let's start first of all concentrating
on the existing customers/owners list.

1   Seek out referral business from existing customers.
    Simply pick up the phone and say something on the
    lines of: 'Listen, Jim, things are a little slow around
    here and I was wondering if you might be able to
    help me out. Can you think of anybody who might
    be interested in . . . ?' They'll help you!

2   Market survey existing customers. Find out if they
    are happy, what if anything would they change and,
    most important, how long they anticipate it will be
    before they renew or replace. Every product or service
    has a lifespan – once you determine what it is, for
    example, three years, contact all customers who are
    approaching the three-year mark.

3   Contact existing customers whenever you have some-
    thing new, e.g. new brochure, new price list, new

product, new discount or sale, new data, new advanced formula, whatever.

4 Almost every business has an after-sales department that deals with customer complaints, replacement parts, repairs and services. Your own service or complaints department can provide you with some excellent leads. Customers with problems are worth their weight in gold!

5 Contact the 'used to be' customers, the ones that all the other salespeople give up on as no-hopers, even if they're not in your area.

6 Take on any customer that another salesperson doesn't want. There are always some that the losers want to get rid of, or give away.

The one that got away
As your customer list continues to grow, so will your repeat business. The next avenue for thought and then ground-work is the list of the 'nearly was' or 'could have beens'.

7 Contact all the old enquiries, the 'could have beens'. These folk obviously had some sparks of interest once. Why not try to rekindle that interest?

8 Get hold of all the company's cancellations, the 'nearly was' list. Most of these ex-customers bought and wobbled because they didn't have a pro-clo like you to service them and to consolidate the deal.

9 Swap your dead leads with those of a colleague or competitor.

From a gentle stream to a mighty flowing river
Then there are endless different lead sources right on your
doorstep. They are like ripe fruit on a tree at harvest-time
– one gentle little tug and they are yours for the taking.

10 Advertise in every newsagent's window in your area.
    If you figure conservatively that each newsagent has
    1,000 customers per week and there are 50 newsagents
    in your area – that's a potential 50,000 prospects
    reading your advert for around £10 per week. Don't
    just use your business card or a normal postcard,
    use something that is eye-catching like a testimonial
    letter from an existing customer.

11 Do the same with each post office window, your local
    garages, video store and the corner shop.

12 Browse through your local newspapers regularly, there
    are always hundreds of potential leads looking you in
    the face. For example, when Mr John Johnson from
    The Street in Anytown raises £1,000 for charity by
    parachuting from a plane – find his address from
    the telephone book. Write congratulating him on his
    performance and enclose your business card, should
    he ever be interested in medical or life insurance. Get
    the idea?

13 Canvass potential customers from your Yellow Pages
    or Thomson Local.

14 Every public library in the land has on its shelves trade
    magazines and publications, business directories and
    company names/addresses, etc., offering a wealth of
    possibilities. There are also guides to almost everything
    imaginable. For example, if you sell salt and pepper

pots, then you'll find guides to hotels, restaurants, public houses, nursing homes, youth hostels, bed and breakfast outlets – the list is endless.

15 Advertise on the noticeboards of the local council offices, community centres, town hall, health and leisure club, the golf club, and so on.

16 Do some cold calling. There is nothing like knocking on a few doors to get the adrenalin pumping. Yes, you get a lot of rejection but you also get success around 10 per cent of the time. If you tell the 'cold calls' that you're in the area and will be calling on such a day or a certain evening (drop a leaflet or brochure through the door), your success rate will be a lot higher than 10 per cent. Ask the Avon lady.

17 Organize an exchange programme with another business (not a competitor) who sells to the same kind of customers you do. As an example, let's take the home improvements industry. Here there is a huge mass of potentially compatible customers from companies that sell such things as double glazing, kitchens, bathrooms, bedrooms, conservatories, security systems, water purifiers, cable television, driveways, patios, textured wall-coating, and so on. You should contact a likely company and arrange to exchange leads or customer lists, like for like.

18 Arrange a direct mail shot or a leaflet drop.

19 Your local estate agents know the names and addresses of hundreds of people who have just moved into new homes. If you sell windows or carpets or water filters or paint, if you sell kitchens or bathrooms or bedrooms

or conservatories, etc. – maybe it might be worth your
while to cross the estate agent's palm with silver, if
business should be generated from any leads he gives
you.

It doesn't stop with estate agents – plumbers know
people who need a new washing machine, mechanics
know customers who are talking about a new car and
vets know of people who are in the market for a new
dog. Be creative!

20 Don't send Christmas cards, send calendars. They
don't have to be expensive or have a different picture
for each month as long as they are attractive and
presentable. Every calendar should have your name,
your company and your telephone numbers on display
in a prominent position. It will be a constant daily
reminder, for the next twelve months, that you are
there for them should they want to upgrade, add
on, replace, or send referrals. For the best impact
and the best results, make your calendar a personal
gift.

There are many other ways of canvassing to generate
new business, but to be effective, be creative, and be
prepared to put in lots of hard work and determined
effort. Here is a little story that demonstrates being creative, taking the initiative and making a determined effort
to canvass my business.

Although I wasn't in any hurry, I'd been considering
for some time making a small conversion to a part of
our home and so I applied for planning permission.
My intention was to save time when I eventually
decided to go ahead and have the work done. I
didn't realize that my application went on public

display at the council offices, but over the next few weeks I received a total of seventeen letters from builders offering their services, builder's merchants pushing their wares, a couple of money-lenders selling finance and even a letter from a company who sold drapery.

At first I was impressed at the initiative these companies had shown in an attempt to canvass my business, but when I looked more closely, I saw a different picture. Only four of the seventeen letters had been signed by their author. The rest were either photocopied signatures informing me it was a standard letter, or they weren't signed at all, or they had been signed 'pp' followed by an illegible scribble. Fifteen of the letters were addressed to Dear Sir, Dear Occupier, or Dear (Space), and six of them said 'date as postmark'.

Only two of the seventeen had bothered to write to me personally, dated their letter and signed it with ink. Of those two only one letter was from a builder, the other was from the draper.

I couldn't help but wonder how many of those seventeen companies would give me the service that I would want. My guess was, only two. As I have explained, I wasn't in any hurry, so I didn't respond to any of the letters. Instead, I just sat on them.

Of those original seventeen, only one bothered to contact me again. Guess which builder it was, and guess who got my business?

The moral of this story is, you must be professional and be personal and you must follow up to follow through.

Recap

We are now about to move on and look at the actual sales process, but before we do let's have a quick refresher.

Step 11   Use ingenuity to pull your customer, not push him.

Step 12   Do your homework and you'll reap the rewards.

Step 13   Canvass, canvass, canvass, then follow up to follow through.

Step 14
The plan of action

A pro-clo always works to a plan of action. He has a strategy, a sequence of events, a proven formula that he follows with each presentation.

Depending upon the product or service there are many adaptations of this plan of action, but a typical sequence of events will run something like this (assuming the appointment has been made).

1   *Meeting/greeting*
     I think it is enough for me to say that nobody gets a second chance to make a first impression. Smile, be friendly, be polite and courteous. Shake hands – get the customer used to it. Remember to take control as soon as possible. Ask the customer to do something: 'Would you come this way?', 'Would you mind turning

the television off', 'Is it all right if I sit here?', and so on.

2   *Setting the scene*
When you first meet a customer, his defence shield, that protective barrier, will be in place to protect him from being sold, to protect him from the unknown. The pro-clo chips away at this barrier until it eventually comes down, until the customer is relaxed and receptive. The best way to start this process is to put your cards on the table and tell the customer what you are going to do. Once you have done this the customer will no longer be afraid of the unknown. You will have made him aware of what is going to happen, and he will start to relax.

If you give the customer an escape route, if you tell him in so many words that you're not going to try and sell him anything and it's OK if he doesn't buy, he will relax that much quicker. I'm not suggesting you let the customer off the hook, I'm suggesting that you imply to the customer that this is what will happen if whatever it is you are selling is not for him. The pro-clo *always* makes the customer want the product, but the customer doesn't know that. The technique of 'Setting the Stage' will be covered in more detail later in this section (Step 16).

3   *Building rapport*
Warm the customer up before moving in to pitch him (Step 18, covered in depth on page 84). This is the crucial stage, the time when the sale can make or break even before the actual presentation. Here, through relaxed conversation (usually with a tea or coffee), the pro-clo builds common bonds, friendship, trust, credibility, warmth, and makes the customer receptive.

4   *Presentation*
Short and simple (covered in Step 20).

5   *Recap*
Once you have made your presentation, recap before
you close to make sure your customer understands
everything and to make sure there are no last-minute
doubts or questions. First, we tell them what we are
going to do, then we do it, then we tell them what
we've just done.

6   *Price/close*
If you don't work from a published price list, hold
back the price until the end. Sell them on what they are
going to get first, then tell them the price. When you go
into a shop to buy a pair of shoes you don't walk in
and ask 'How much are your shoes?'. You look first,
then when you're interested you find out the price.
The price should always be held until last because if
the customer knows the price before he knows what
he is going to get for the price, the chances are he
will put his blinkers on. He will decide he can't afford
it before he has seen what it will do for him. When
this happens the customer will not be listening to the
presentation, he has already decided. It is impossible
to close a door that has not been opened, so don't give
the customer a price until you are ready, until you've
opened the door. Keep control.
   If the customer continually asks: 'So what does it
cost? How much is it? When are you going to tell me
the price? Look, tell me what I want to know, how
much?', you cannot continually keep fobbing him off
without his becoming irritated. The best way to handle
this situation without aggravating him is to say something on the lines of: 'Mr Jones, it could work out to

be anything from £2 a day (which intimates finance) to a one-off £200,000 depending on the size, the location, the quantity, the grading, and so on. It is impossible for me to give you a realistic or accurate figure until we've decided whether or not this (*product*) would suit you, and if so, then how many, where, when, etc. – please, bear with me a while longer.' *Occasionally* and I emphasize that, occasionally, with a very awkward customer, give him the price, otherwise you will lose him and you don't want to do that until you've given it your best shot, do you?

Summary

Meeting – Setting the stage – Building rapport – Presentation – Recap – Price – Close.

This is the basic plan of action and any other sequence, strategy, or formula (call it what you like) takes this basic plan and adds to it, maybe with a tour, a demonstration, a film, and so on. At the end of the day it is a plan of action, and in our next step we will look at how it works.

Step 15
How it works

Customers buy emotionally and justify their decision with logic.

At the beginning of a sales presentation, the customer is at an emotional low. By following the plan of action, the proven success formula, the pro-clo gradually brings the customer from that low point to the emotional high where the customer is sold. This is the time to close.

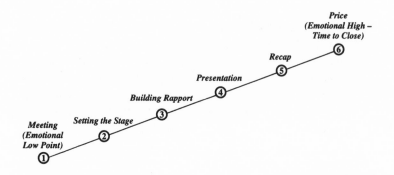

Let's suppose, on the other hand, that the pro-clo didn't follow the basic plan of action – then this is what would happen.

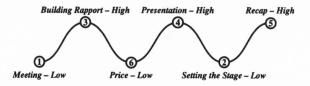

Instead of a smooth gradual climb towards the summit, the closer plays with the customer's emotions. One minute he is up, the next he is down – in the end the poor old customer is so confused and emotionally drained that he can't decide, he just has to 'think about it'!

Follow the plan of action – it's a set procedure that has evolved over years and years of successful selling.

Let me give you another analogy to show you how it works. First, another quick recap of the basic plan of action.

1 Meeting/greeting
2 Setting the stage
3 Building rapport
4 Presentation
5 Recap
6 Price/close.

Imagine you are on holiday, you are lying on a beach sunbathing and generally having a good time. A few feet away a couple are doing the same. As you are both staying in the same hotel you recognize each other, and after the 'knowing nod' and an occasional smile, you start chatting.

(MEETING/GREETING) 'How long are you here for? Have you been before? Have you tried the restaurant yet? . . . Listen, in a while, when I've finished reading the paper, I was going to swim out to that yacht over there. Why don't you join me? It belongs to a friend of mine and he allows me to take her out whenever I'm down here.

(SETTING THE STAGE) 'We could just go out for half an hour or so, not too far – I'll show you the coastline and we could maybe have lunch. In fact, it would be nice to have some company, but if you don't like it, or as soon as you've had enough (*if it's not for you*), I'll bring you straight back, fair enough?

(BUILDING RAPPORT) 'Have you ever done any sailing before? Really? If you don't mind my saying, you've got a great physique. How often do you work out? . . . Let's go dip our feet and see how the water is.

(PRESENTATION) 'Come on in a little bit deeper. Don't worry, it's not cold – the beach is only there, you can always turn around! Hey, look at that, feel this, come on, let's go in a little further – first one past their belly button!'

The customer objects: 'It's too cold, I think I might be getting a little out of my depth, maybe this wasn't such a good idea after all.' He looks over his shoulder towards the beach, he's now up to his waist and he needs a little reassurance.

'Come on, look at everyone else enjoying themselves, look, they're swimming and see how happy they are. We'll just wade out a little farther, then if you want to turn back we will, but we've come this far, we may as well get our hair wet. Come on a little more, a little more, that's it, you're doing great. Now let go, take your feet off the ground, let the buoyancy take over and you'll be swimming.

(RECAP) 'The yacht is only there. In ten minutes we could be off around the headland – we'll have fresh fish and salad for lunch. Now that we're up to our necks, there's no point standing on our tiptoes and bobbing up and down with the swells.

(PRICE) 'Let go – go on, you can do it, you'll feel great.' The customer is in too deep to change his mind – again he looks over his shoulder towards the beach, but now it's a long way away.

(CLOSE) 'We're almost there, it'll take us two minutes – swim now.'

The customer hesitates. He is still bobbing up and down, so you put your hand out to beckon him. The customer sees the wave, he feels it and it's too powerful to resist, so he reaches out to take your hand and as he does he is lifted off the floor.

(CLOSED) The customer is now swimming happily towards (*his benefits*) the yacht and there's a great big smile on his face.

Follow the plan of action. It is a natural smooth incline,

a gradual build-up, with no pregnant pauses or dramatic turn-arounds. The pro-clo gently creeps up on his customers, he puts his arm around them, he reassures them, he persuades and convinces and cajoles them towards owning his product.

Step 16
Setting the stage (the pact)

Once the pro-clo has introduced himself to his customer (assuming it's a confirmed appointment), he will immediately proceed to set the stage for the sales presentation. The pro-clo basically lays his cards on the table and makes a pact with the customer.

The pro-clo knows that when they first meet, the customer is cold (although he may not appear so). His defence shield is well and truly in place – it's like a brick wall guarding the customer from the unknown and protecting himself from being sold.

Before any niceties such as tea, coffee, or chit-chat, the pro-clo sets the stage and explains exactly what is going to happen. In doing so he makes the customer aware – and so the customer's fear of the unknown begins to subside and the defence shield starts to come down. This makes the next part of the sales procedure, the warm-up period, the building of rapport, so much easier.

Setting the stage or forming a pact also helps eliminate customer procrastination at closing time. Here's an example of what to say (adapt it to your own situation).

'Mr Jones, before we start, I'd like to take a couple
of seconds to maybe clear the air and explain what
I'm going to do. First of all, I'm going to explain
all about our (*product*), we're going to see all of its
benefits and I'm going to show you how it works. At
the end, when I've shown and explained everything
to you, I'll ask you for a simple yes or no . . . If
you like it, you want one and it's yes, then you will
join our many thousands of satisfied customers, but
on the other hand, if it's no, please don't worry
about it, I'll still shake your hand, and we'll still
be friends . . . fair enough?' (Smile warmly and
nod your head in agreement.)

The majority of customers will agree and say 'OK' – then
you can almost see them start to relax. The reason for this
is that the pro-clo has just given them an escape route, a
way out – they feel that they are not committed or obligated
and all they have to say at the end of the day is 'No, thank
you'. The pro-clo won't be upset if they don't buy. He even
said they would remain friends and shake hands.

This technique makes the customer so much more receptive. Of course this is only a tactic to get the customer's
guard down and it's the pro-clo's job to make sure the
customer is obligated.

Sometimes however, the customer will respond with a
minor objection (discussed in more detail in Part Two on
page 151). Here are a few common ones.

(a) 'That's fine, but just how long is this going to take?'
(b) 'No matter what you show me or how much it costs,
    I won't make a decision today.'
(c) 'We're in the middle of moving house (or changing
    jobs, or being made redundant), so I don't think we
    will be buying.'

(d) 'We're only looking for our son (partner, friends, etc.).'
(e) 'I'm interested, but I don't want to waste your time – I just couldn't afford to do anything at this present time.'
(f) 'That's great – I'm actually in the market to buy, so I don't need to go through all the sales patter – just show me and give me a price. If I like it, I'll buy it!'

At the beginning of the presentation, the customer who throws out these minor objections does so for one reason – he is scared of being sold, so he tries to throw the pro-clo off-balance. It's the customer's way of saying 'Don't try to sell to me, because I'm not buying'. These minor objections should just be ignored, because they are never real. When someone tells you 'No matter what you show me or how much it costs, I won't make a decision today', if you read between the lines and translate what they are saying, it means that they are scared of doing just that, making a decision. It also tells you that they are in a position (financially) to make the decision, because what they said was, they won't (not can't) decide today. (Translating objections is covered in more detail in Part Two on page 147.)

No matter what the customer says, no matter how ridiculous an objection may seem *never, ever, argue*. Don't let the customer sell you.

This is how the pro-clo would respond to the above examples.

(a) 'Not long at all, and I'll be as quick as I can.' (This statement lets the customer feel that he has thrown the pro-clo off the scent and so he starts to relax. His defence shield begins to come down and the customer becomes more receptive. Of course, the pro-clo continues at normal speed.)

(b) 'Mr Jones, that's fine, all I ask is that you keep an
    open mind, is that fair enough?'
(c) 'Well, I certainly hope that everything works out for
    you – all I ask is that you keep an open mind, you
    might be pleasantly surprised.'
(d) 'That's fine, we do a tremendous amount of business
    from referrals . . . but would you do me a favour?
    Would you keep an open mind as if you were looking
    for yourselves . . . see whether or not you personally
    would like to own this (*product*)? If you would, great,
    if not, then there is no harm done. Fair enough?'
(e) 'Well, I'm sorry to hear that, Mr Jones, but as you're
    interested . . . I'll show you everything anyway and
    leave you to make up your own mind, OK?'
(f) 'Certainly, Mr Jones . . . However, there are a few
    things about this (*product*) that are unique, so I'll take
    the time to explain them to you as quickly as possible,
    OK?' (The pro-clo then follows his plan of action at
    the normal speed and doesn't miss anything out.)

It's important that you 'set the stage' as quickly as
possible after the initial greeting. I've known salespeople
who warm their customers up, create the friendly, warm,
receptive atmosphere first, and then set the stage. When
this happens, the customer sees a friend turning back into
a salesperson, the protective defence shield comes back
into action again and the salesperson has made his job
that much harder.

Set the stage early, get it out of the way. Then start the
gradual, smooth climb, towards the emotional high point,
when the customer (who started out just window shopping)
is so involved and enthusiastic and committed he just can't
say no!

Step 17
Be a good listener

Unlike most salespeople, a pro-clo is a good listener. He knows the 'two ears and one mouth' rule, so he listens twice as much as he speaks. Selling is not so much the 'gift of the gab' or 'having the spiel' but more the ability to listen and hear. A pro-clo is constantly listening for the customer's wants, needs, aspirations and desires, he is constantly listening and gathering pertinent information to help close the sale. He is listening for possible objections and even subconsciously listening for distractions, such as an awkward customer nearby or a loud salesperson spouting off to someone else. A pro-clo especially listens to what his customer is not saying.

A friend of mine who runs a very successful international sales company uses the following technique when recruiting to find a good listener.

In a hotel conference room, with maybe a hundred prospective candidates applying for a sales job, the interviewer stands in front of his audience and explains that for the next five minutes he will inform them about the company's history and the company's products. He asks them to please pay attention and then commences.

Two or three minutes into the introduction, this set-up occurs. A man enters the room, walks towards the front, and stops by an empty table in the corner opposite the interviewer. Without looking at the audience, and without saying a word, the stranger begins putting plates on the table.

The interviewer completely ignores the man, he doesn't even glance at him or acknowledge that he is there – he just continues talking as if nothing is happening. The stranger, meanwhile, takes a can of shaving cream, shakes it vigorously and then starts to fill the plates with cream.

The audience become bewildered and somewhat amused. Once all the plates are brimming over, the stranger leaves the room, again without saying a word. The interviewer continues for another 30 seconds or so, then he instructs the candidates to write down answers to the simple questions he is about to ask, on what he has just explained.

The vast majority of the audience are unable to do this, as they weren't listening to the interviewer. Instead, they were distracted by the stranger and were paying more attention to him. However, there are always a small handful who are able to answer the simple questions and thus prove that they were not distracted and were in fact listening. These handful either already are or turn out to be professional closers.

Remember, nobody likes to be ignored. Or put another way, everyone loves to be heard (and heard out, without interruption).

How to Become a Good Listener
1   Make listening enjoyable by taking a sincere interest in what your customers are saying. Force your mind not to wander.

2   Don't ever assume that you know what your customer is about to say, because this will break your concentration and you won't listen attentively.

3   Don't simply listen to what your customer is saying (in one ear and out the other). Understand it and take it in. This is the only way you can satisfy a customer need.

4   Make your customer the most important thing on your mind.

5   Listening, especially when you want to talk or you are distracted, is very difficult. Learn to restrain yourself.

6   Always keep eye contact with your customer, look for facial expressions and listen for voice inflection. Often, actions speak louder than words. A pro-clo learns to listen with his eyes.

7   If you write down pertinent information from your customer it will help you to listen more attentively and remember what was said.

8   Don't always take what your customer says at face value. Question your customer's statements.

9   Don't interrupt a customer, or cut him short, unless he is being negative.

10   Remember, customers love to talk, especially about themselves. The more they talk, the more comfortable they feel, and the more they will open up to you. Everyone loves a good listener, so listen.

Listening requires concentration and patience.

Now read these two sentences aloud. Which do you think is correct?

(a) The yolk of an egg *is* white.
(b) The yolk of an egg *are* white.

If you get it right, congratulations, you are an excellent listener. If you get it wrong, you've got some practising to do. The answer is at the foot of the next page.

Step 18
Building rapport (warm-up)

There are no ifs, buts, or maybes about it – without any shadow of a doubt, the most important part of any sales call or presentation is the *warm-up* session, that period of time for building rapport. There is always the odd exception but generally, people will not buy off you if they don't like you. How many people have you ever sold to that didn't like you? In all likelihood, your answer will be 'None'.

Customers come in all different shapes and sizes, all different ages and religions. They come in different appearances and from different social classes, they come with different forms of intelligence and in more than just two sexes. Have you ever wondered why it is that some salespeople can only sell to a certain category of customer? The reason is that they haven't learnt or acquired the technique of being able to react to, and blend in with, all individual customers. They only sell to the ones they can relate to more easily.

This period of 'warming-up' the customer or building rapport has a number of objectives that can either make or break the sale, before the presentation has even started.

Let's now look at a few of those objectives and the reasons why they are so very important.

1 *Establish rapport* so that the customer warms to you and enjoys your company. Once a rapport has been established the customer will start to feel obligated towards you and he will not want to let you down.

2 *Relax the customer* to bring the customer's defence shield down and create a receptive environment. If the customer is up-tight and his defence shield remains intact, he will not listen or get involved in the presentation – instead he will concentrate on protecting himself.

3 *Develop trust* so that your customer believes in you, your product and your company.

4 *Gather information* so that you can find out the pertinent information needed to help you close the sale.

5 *Establish common ground* so that you relate to each other and get on well together. This makes the customer more favourable towards you.

6 *Create a bond* so that the customer feels obligated and loyal to you. This creates a personal relationship, which ensures the sale stays sold and also encourages the customer to give you repeat and referral business.

(The answer is neither. The yolk of an egg is yellow, not white).

7   *Boost his ego.* If you put the customer on a pedestal,
    if you boost his ego and make him feel good about
    himself, he will also feel good about you.

8   *Create a receptive environment* so that the customer
    is relaxed. If the customer likes you and enjoys your
    company, he will be more attentive and receptive to
    your presentation.

The more effective the 'warm-up', the easier it is to make
the sale. A lay-down (an easy sale) results from an excellent
warm-up. Depending upon your sales situation, there is
no definite period of time as to how long the 'warm-up'
should last. It could be two minutes, or ten minutes,
or a week, or even a year. Generally speaking, in the
field of direct sales to qualified but cold leads, a typical
warm-up period would last 30 minutes before the pro-clo
would move into his presentation.

Although no two customers are the same, all customers,
being human, have certain characteristics that respond to
the efforts of the pro-clo to warm them up. In his book
How To Win Customers and Keep Them For Life, Michael
LeBoeuf gives some useful tips for establishing rapport. I
have used a selection of them in compiling the following
list.

Useful Tips for Building Rapport

1   Develop a genuine interest in the customer, not just
    in his money.

2   Find some common ground, e.g. if the customer was
    in the army, then you were in the army, or your
    father was, or your brother is, and so on. Be truthful,

otherwise you will be caught out and you will lose your credibility.

3   Compliment and praise the customer sincerely but not too frequently, otherwise it will become obvious that you are stroking his ego.

4   Make the customer laugh, get him to have a good time, but don't make a fool of yourself.

5   Smile often and from your eyes – smiling just from your mouth looks sarcastic and false. (A genuine smile creates folds of skin under the eyes – try it!)

6   Encourage the customer to talk about himself – everyone loves to do that. You will be amazed at the amount of information you will pick up.

7   Maintain eye contact – it shows sincerity.

8   Use the customer's name frequently – it will create warmth and a closeness – but not so frequently that it becomes annoying.

9   Make a pact with the customer. Tell him exactly what you are going to do – alleviate his fear of the unknown and bring down his defence barrier (see Step 16).

10   There are only two kinds of people who fall for flattery – men and women. Use it.

11   Mirror image the customer positively. When he smiles, you smile, when he laughs, you laugh, when he is telling a story and acts surprised, you act surprised.

12 Tell the customer a secret. Take him into your confidence, make the relationship a personal one.

13 Volunteer personal information about yourself and you will encourage the customer to do the same.

14 Tell the customer an emotional story, be it happy or sad, and use lots of emotion to illustrate. Customers love to feel that they really know you, personally.

15 Make a commitment to the customer, e.g. a dinner date or a golf match, and keep it. This makes the customer feel ever more obligated.

16 Be polite and courteous at all times.

17 Subtly touch, but in a non-offensive manner, and not too often.

18 It's flattering to be asked for advice, so ask for it.

19 We all relate to people who are like us or aspire to be, so be like your customer.

20 Remember that you have two ears and one mouth. Use them in that proportion.

The warm-up is, without question, the most important part of the sales presentation. High-pressure, bulldozer closers do close sales, but it is the closer who builds rapport with his customer who keeps it sold, and gets repeat business, and gets referrals. Do unto others as you would have others do unto yourself.

My brother-in-law, George, is a partner in a firm of

builder's merchants in London. Talk about competition, there are some 250 merchants in the London area, and they all sell exactly the same products for almost exactly the same price. They all buy their goods from the same manufacturer and they are all out to try and service the same accounts. This is the ultimate competition, 250+ suppliers, selling the same products to the same customers for the same price, even with the same delivery service, the same periods of credit and the same after-sales service.

How, then, does George manage to outshine the rest? How does he, day in, day out, year after year, beat the competition? The answer is simply: George's ability to warm people up, to build rapport, is superb. I have never met anyone who doesn't like George, or who could say a wrong word against him, and that includes the competition (although some have tried). George doesn't cold call as such, because he has an established customer base, and in the building field new customers don't appear overnight, they evolve over years – but he is forever calling just the same. He has over 500 customers and he knows everything about them, their wives' and children's names, where they live and what their interests are, and so on. They get birthday cards, Christmas presents and meals on their anniversary. No! I'm going to contradict myself, George doesn't have over 500 customers, he has over 500 friends who just happen also to be customers. And his biggest asset – he is one of the best listeners I've ever met.

If you have an effective warm-up, your customers will want to buy, and buy again, and supply you with referrals and testimonials.

That's one of the biggest secrets of the pro-clo! Now

just for good measure, give another genuine smile, so those folds of skin appear under your eyes. Feels good, doesn't it?

Recap

Step 14   Always work to a plan of action.

Step 15   Understand how it works. The climb to the emotional high point is a gradual one.

Step 16   Set the stage for your customer and allay his fear of the unknown.

Step 17   Remember the two ears and one mouth rule. Listen to your customer and hear what he is saying.

Step 18   Build a good rapport and you're halfway there.

Step 19
KISS it (Keep It Short and Sweet)

A pro-clo is continually updating his product knowledge. He knows literally everything about his company, his products and services. Very rarely will a pro-clo say 'I don't know' – unless he has ulterior motives.

If the ingredients of the sale are 95 per cent enthusiasm and only 5 per cent product knowledge, why is it important for the pro-clo to be such an expert on product knowledge? The answer is that a pro-clo must be able to answer any question that a customer asks without hesitation, and a pro-clo must be competent enough to know specifics when required. Having superior product knowledge makes the pro-clo the professional he is, it makes him confident and gives him total belief in his product, so much so that it generates the all-important enthusiasm.

Although the pro-clo is an expert on his product, he does not volunteer all this information to each client because he knows that not only would he bore them to death, he would also confuse them.

The pro-clo keeps his presentation short and sweet and straight to the point. It is a very simple presentation, only mentioning the most pertinent of points, and being somewhat repetitive to make sure the customer understands each owner benefit.

The more information a client is given, the more likely it is he will have to think about it. Occasionally, a pro-clo will deliberately miss out pertinent information from his presentation, so that he can bring it up at the end and bring pressure to bear, e.g. 'Oh, how stupid of me, I forgot to mention . . .' or 'Do you remember, Mr Jones, that you wanted this (*benefit*)? Well, I've been saving the best until last . . .'

KISS it. You can always add a little more information, but you can't take it away once you've spilled your guts out and bored them to tears with triviality.

Step 20

The presentation

'Tell me, I'll forget – show me, I might remember – but involve me, and I'll understand.'

It amazes me that some sales organizations still insist that all new recruits learn a canned pitch, verbatim, word for word. This simply does not work, because the presentation or pitch must be adapted to each individual customer. No two closers are alike, and if you try to present your product using someone else's words it will sound insincere and false and out of character, and it will sound exactly what it is, a 'canned pitch'. Learn from other people, certainly. If you like how somebody else says something, use it. But most important, use your own personality.

Remember, the presentation should be light and entertaining (KISS it). Use your voice, hands, face and pen, as well as your sales aids and any other tools at your disposal, to keep the customer's attention and interest.

The presentation must be somewhat repetitive, so that the pertinent points (the owner benefits) become embedded in the customer's subconscious. Then he will remember them when it is time to buy. The pro-clo knows his presentation inside out and back to front, but he understands that this will be the first time his customer will have heard it. So each presentation is like the first time – full of enthusiasm and excitement and involvement.

It is said that a picture is worth a thousand words – there is much truth in this statement. We also remember a lot more from what we see than from what we hear.

It stands to reason, then, that the majority of the presentation should be visual. If you use graphs or charts, keep them very simple and very easy to read. All customers have short attention spans, so don't bore them with details or trivia, concentrate on the stuff that sells your product and KISS it.

Never say 'If you own', say 'When you own', and the customer begins to assume that he does in fact, own.

If you are selling to a couple, be aware of how you seat them. The pro-clo knows that the less distance there is between himself and customers, the more control he will have. This is the best seating arrangement there is.

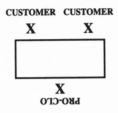

Try to arrange the seating so that everyone is an equal distance from each other. The seating arrangement illustrated above allows the pro-clo to maintain eye contact with both customers, whereas any other seating arrangement forces the pro-clo to play tennis (from one side of the court to the other and then back again). This not only gives you neck-ache, but allows one customer to communicate with the other when you're looking the other way.

When selling on the customer's home turf, never sit in the customer's seat or chair, instead wait to be invited to sit down. When it's time to make your presentation, politely suggest that you use the desk or kitchen table and then follow the same seating procedure as described above.

As we have already mentioned, a pro-clo knows his presentation inside out and back to front. He is so conversant that he could sell his product with his eyes closed and read his literature upside-down – and on this latter point, that is exactly what he does. A pro-clo turns his literature and materials around so that they are facing his customer, then, using his pen to guide him, he will read any important piece upside-down. The customer then takes in what is being said more easily, because we all remember more from what we see than from what we hear.

Professional closers personalize their presentations to each individual customer. They also involve their customers: try this, feel that, listen to it, smell this one. A good way of keeping the customer involved is by using tie-downs (discussed in detail in Step 30), or by partially stating something and having the customer automatically finish the sentence. For instance 'A picture is worth . . . ?' (Pause, raise your eyebrows and nod.)

Summary

1   Always use your own personality when making a presentation, never try to be someone else.

2   KISS it.

3   Use your voice, hands, face, pen, and visual sales aids.

4   Repeat the pertinent points and recap at the end.

5   Be enthusiastic.

6   Involve the customer.

7   Be more visual than verbal whilst presenting your product.

8   Use 'when', rather than 'if'.

9   Be aware of how you seat your customers for the presentation.

10 Always have any literature, materials, etc., facing your customers. Use your pen as a pointer and read upside-down.

Step 21
Financial logic (building value)

Regardless of the product or service, every presentation must have a certain amount of financial logic to it. The product must make financial sense to the customer, if he is to justify purchasing it and if it's to remain sold.

Remember that most of what we take in is through our eyes, so when explaining the financial logic of your product – be visual. Use simple, easy-to-follow graphs or charts or testimonials, etc., to prove your case. Demonstrate how your product will save the customer money or how it will appreciate in value. At the end of the day, the customer must feel that the product will give him value for money – the benefits that he (the customer) will derive from the product must be worth more to him than the money it costs to purchase it.

Whenever you work out figures with your customer, use a calculator and show the customer the window, hold it up to him. This little technique gives credibility to your calculations (machines don't lie) and the customer is more likely to remember a figure that he both sees and hears.

Building Value

When someone buys an expensive bottle of perfume or aftershave, although it doesn't save the customer money, or appreciate in value, the benefit the customer envisages from the sensual aroma is worth more than the money it costs to purchase. This, in the customer's mind, is value for money.

The value of a product is in direct proportion to the amount of customer benefits that will be derived from owning the product. The more benefits, the more value. Once the value of a product has reached a certain level, it will be worth more to the customer than the money it costs to purchase it. However, be careful not to oversell. Every salesperson will have experienced a situation where the customer says 'Is that all it costs?' or 'What's the catch?' and the favourite response to oversell, 'It sounds too good to be true!' Timing when to close is a crucial step in any sale and we shall be looking at this in detail in Step 33.

Recap

Step 19   KISS it. Keep your presentation short and simple and straight to the point.

Step 20   Involve your customers in the presentation. Be visual, enthusiastic and somewhat repetitive with the owner benefits.

Step 21   Using benefits, build value but be careful not to oversell.

Step 22
Verbal communication

Many sales books or sales trainers teach us that there are certain words that we should avoid like the plague when we are selling. For example:

We don't say 'buy', we say 'invest' or 'own'
We don't say 'deposit', we say 'initial investment'
We don't say 'contract', we say 'agreement' or 'paperwork'
We don't say 'sign', we say 'approve this', etc.

Whilst I agree with the principles of these positive selling words against those frightening negative ones, I believe that far too much importance is given to this line of thinking. I don't believe that a single word such as 'buy' or 'sign' will stop a customer from purchasing. One single word would not stop a pro-clo from making the sale, but eliminating negative words and replacing them with softer, more positive words does make his job easier.

The American sales trainer Hank Trisler, in his book *No Bull Selling*, tells the tale of how he once got caught up with these positive selling words and how he had to revert back to basics. Here it is as it's written:

I'd say, 'Tell me, Mr and Mrs Gorman, what portion of your savings have you set aside for your initial investment?'

They'd look at each other blankly, then look at me and chime, in unison, 'Huh?'

Then I'd have to say, 'If you were to scrape it all

together and put it all in one pile; money, marbles and chalk, how many bucks you got to put down on this shack, Jack?'

This passage certainly proves the point that communicating to a customer is not about what you say but rather *how* you say it. Selling is a very personal business and the only way you will communicate to your customers is by being personal and being yourself.

There are many other ways of communicating to customers but our voice is one of the most powerful selling tools we have. The way we speak, the way we place emphasis on certain words, is called voice inflection. This enables us to communicate effectively and put our message across to our customers.

Hank Trisler and Zig Ziglar both give some excellent examples of using voice inflection. Borrowing their common idea, I have developed an example of my own, using this statement: 'He didn't say he couldn't do it.'

Now, using voice inflection, read the following five sentences aloud – emphasize the words in capital letters and you will give the sentence five different meanings.

1   HE didn't say he couldn't do it. (This implies that someone else said it.)

2   He DIDN'T say he couldn't do it. (It's a lie.)

3   He didn't SAY he couldn't do it. (He didn't actually say it, but that's what he meant.)

4   He didn't say HE couldn't do it. (He can do it, it's somebody else that can't.)

5   He didn't say he COULDN'T do it. (Of course he
can, but will he?)

A pro-clo uses voice inflection all the time – it's a great
way of demonstrating a point, of keeping interest, of
emphasizing and asking questions without asking directly.
So when a customer says 'It costs too much', the pro-clo,
using voice inflection, echoes the statement back: 'It costs
TOO MUCH?' The statement becomes a question and the
customer has to either justify himself or back down.

As well as voice inflection or emphasizing certain words,
there are many other features of our voice that we can
improve upon or use to benefit our presentation.

Accent
If you have a strong accent, don't try to change it. People
are intrigued by an accent, it causes them to listen more
carefully and concentrate more on what is being said.

Still on the subject of accents, for a little fun see if
you can decipher this message:

'Si Señor, der dago, forte lorez inero.' – 'Dernot lorez,
demar trux fulla cowz en ens un dux.'

(Translated, the above becomes: 'Si Señor, there they
go, forty lorries in a row.' – 'They're not lorries, them
are trucks full of cows and hens and ducks.')

Volume
Vary the volume of your voice throughout the presentation. Not only will this stop your customer from falling
asleep, it will keep the flow alive. Talking loudly creates excitement and confidence, whereas whispering brings
people closer together.

Tone/Pitch

Can you think of anything more boring than listening to someone with a one-pitch/monotone voice rambling on and on like the hum of an engine. Change the pitch of your voice, from deep for credibility to high for surprise, excitement, or pleasure. People generally equate a deep voice with sincerity and credibility. How about the singer Barry White, or the chap on the television who does the Mr Kipling adverts, 'exceedingly good!'. The deep voice suggests credibility, so much so that you want to run out to the late night store and buy a packet of Mr Kipling fruit fancies.

Speed

Alternating the speed of your speech will optimize the attention of your customer. Speak quickly to create excitement and enthusiasm – speak more slowly to emphasize a point and create credibility. (When speaking quickly, be careful not to lose your customer or start babbling.)

In many instances, it is not what you say that creates the impression, but the way that you say it. We've all heard, or know of somebody who has, what is termed a 'telephone voice'. These people tend to pronounce their words with more clarity or put on another voice when speaking over a telephone. In many cases, although the telephone voice is intentional, the speaker is completely oblivious to the change. When these people are speaking face to face, they use lots of body language to communicate – and when the body language is restricted because of a telephone, they automatically revert to 'speech language' to convey their desired impression.

Practise communicating with your voice, it's one of the most powerful tools that we all possess.

Step 23
Emotive words open doors

There are many words that have strong connotations which are very influential when selling. The use of these decisive words helps to create positive emotions in your customers, which makes it easier to make the sale.

There are literally hundreds of these positive emotive words, but I'm just going to mention a few of the most popular. You should use them liberally throughout your presentation.

SECURITY	HAPPINESS
PEACE OF MIND	PLEASURE
INVESTMENT	LUXURY
VALUE	EXCITEMENT
FUN	STRENGTH
JOY	HEALTH
PRIDE	LOVE

Research has shown the fifteen most persuasive words in the English language are:

IMPROVE	GAIN
REDUCE	DISCOVERY
RESULTS	EASY
SAVE	YOU
INCREASE	GUARANTEE
PROVEN	MONEY
HAVE	SAFE . . .

. . . and by far the best, the most persuasive word in selling, is the word NEW. A new service, a new product, a new promotion, a new brochure, a new model will open many doors that would otherwise remain closed. All you have to do to get customers is hang a great big sign over your stall that says NEW.

Step 24
Descriptive words paint pictures that come to life

Using descriptive words is like painting a picture to the customer, a picture of how things are going to be. A friend and a pro-clo of many years, Paul Stewart, suggests that one of the best examples of painting pictures with descriptive words can be found in travel brochures. I agree. When most people book their holidays, they do so after browsing through travel brochures in the comfort of their own home. The tour operators don't have salespeople to sell their holidays for them, at least not in the customer's home, so they rely on the customers to sell themselves, through descriptive words and pictures. Some of these brochures are so elaborate and so effective that you can picture the scene, you can taste and smell and hear as if you were actually there.

Look at these two examples.

Set amid the warm currents of the crystal clear Java Sea, the island is lush with tropical growth and green-ery. Unlike any other destination in the world, the peaceful tranquillity conjures up dreams of romance as the gentle surf breaks upon the beaches of soft white sand . . .

The air is so clean and fresh and cool and the only sounds are the whispering of the breeze and your own footsteps crunching in the crisp white snow. The sweet aroma of the pine trees, damp with dew, lingers in the valley . . .

Selling is simply creating emotion, and good descriptive words will paint the picture for your customer. For example, if you sell bathrooms, they are not just nice bathrooms – they are bright and clean and fresh-sh-sh!, the tiles are warm and they reflect the natural light like a mirror, the pastel-coloured bath is deep and moulded to the contours of your body for comfort and relaxation, and so on.

When all is said and done a pro-clo is a dream merchant. He creates and sells dreams and, using descriptive words, he brings the dream to life.

Note
One of the best ways to learn how to communicate, express yourself and be good with words, is to enrol on a public speaking course.

Step 25
Non-verbal communication (body language)

As the saying goes, 'Actions speak louder than words'. Actions are also more effective when selling.

We have already looked at a few ways that we

communicate to customers without saying a word. Let's have a quick recap before we look at others.

The way we dress and smell and groom ourselves, and the way we look after our records and selling materials, demonstrates to our customers our professionalism. The way we listen to and show an interest in our customers communicates our sincerity, concern and warmth. The way we point and tap things with our pen somewhat mesmerizes the customers, it keeps their attention and helps demonstrate our presentation and keep control.

By far the most effective ways of communicating to customers are with an entertaining visual demonstration (or presentation) and with body language. Body language plays a big part in communication and in particular the face and facial expressions are superb at convincing the customer and getting him involved and committed.

A pro-clo is a good actor and a good actor is able to express himself so that his audience understand and feel emotion as they follow the story. An actor, like the pro-clo, makes his audience feel part of the story using not only words, but also actions involving his body, hands and face. You touch somebody to show warmth and encouragement, you smile to show friendship and to be pleasant, you use your hand in a sweeping gesture to beckon your customer to sit or to come forward, and so on.

The face is a marvellous selling tool. It has a mirror-like effect on the customer – it's almost like monkey see, monkey do. Ever tried grinning to break the ice? Instead of speaking, just sit there with a great big stupid grin on your face and give an occasional chuckle – I guarantee the customer will be right there with you, before long.

Nod when you're talking and people automatically agree with you and nod back without realizing it. (Nod gently and discreetly, not up and down and from side to side like one of those toy dogs in the back window of a Cortina.)

Pull your eyebrows down and people will automatically justify or explain in detail what they have just said. Yawn and everyone else yawns, laugh and everyone laughs, jump (become startled) unexpectedly and everyone jumps – it even works with calls of nature (that's why so many women follow each other to the toilets).

Everyone uses body language, practically all day long, but most people aren't conscious or aware of it. The pro-clo however, is aware – he learns not only how to use body language to express himself when he is selling, but also how to read his customer's body language (as we shall see in more detail in Step 33).

Practise expressing yourself to another person or in front of the mirror. The better you become at it, the better your sales figures will look.

Everyone who manages other people, and every salesperson who wants to succeed, should learn how to read body language. One of the best books I have read on the subject is *The Secret Language of Success* by Dr David Lewis, and the following exercise is an adaptation of an extract taken from his book.

For a little fun and good practice, try this exercise with your colleagues. Using only body language (no talking), try to communicate or express the following:

1 Express happiness, surprise, confusion and excitement.

2 Command somebody to come here, to sit down, to stand up, to go away.

3 Tell somebody to be quiet, to speak up, to follow, to calm down.

4 Inform somebody it's OK, tell them you agree, tell them you disagree.

5   Indicate money first, say come on let's go, or how
    about a lift?

6   Express he's got a screw loose, it's suicidal, and express
    that something is extremely funny.

Most of the signs for the above instructions are univer-
sally understood. You should be able to communicate these
messages effectively, and likewise you should be able to
communicate your message effectively to your customers.
One more time, most of what we remember comes from
what we see. Not only should your presentation be more
visual than verbal, but so too should your speech. Your
speech should be more visual than verbal.

Recap: Recipe for Effective Communication

Step 22   Use your voice inflection and vary the volume,
          tone and speed of your speech.

Step 23   Add a dozen or so tablespoons of emotive words.

Step 24   Blend together with some good descriptive words
          and bring to the boil.

Step 25   Sprinkle the mixture generously with body lan-
          guage and finally, for good measure, top it off
          with a dusting of enthusiasm.

Note
For best results, serve warm, and dish it up by bringing
the human senses into play (next step).

Step 26
The six human senses (5 + 1)

It has been said that man supposedly lost his sixth sense as he progressed from primitive man. This might be true of most people, but not the pro-clo. You see, professional closers still have their sixth sense, it's an animal-like awareness called instinct or the ability to perceive. The longer you are in this profession, the more acute this sixth sense, this perception, becomes.

It's almost as if a pro-clo were able to read the future or determine the outcome of a particular event, but in reality, this perception evolves from the inner faith a pro-clo has in himself – in his ability to manipulate his own mind and that of other people through PMA (positive mental attitude).

A pro-clo uses all his six senses when he is with a customer, especially his perception, his awareness of the customer's feelings. What, then (for those of us who have forgotten), are the five human senses? They are the ability to see, hear, taste, smell and touch.

When the pro-clo is at work, he tries to bring into play as many of the customer's senses as possible (just like the travel brochures selling the holidays) to help create the all-important emotions needed to close the sale.

As always, the best way to illustrate is by way of example. We will stay on the theme of holidays and endeavour to bring the senses into play. Using your hands and facial expressions and also your voice inflection, express yourself whilst reading the following examples aloud.

See
Try to picture this. Soft white sand, the pale blue Caribbean sea as still as a mill pond, there's a sailing boat

gliding across the horizon and the sun is an orange globe as it starts its descent. Along the coastline there is an abundance of palm trees, tall and erect with masses of green foliage, swaying gently.

Hear

Be quiet and listen carefully. Imagine putting a large shell to your ear. Can you hear the ocean and the occasional crashing of the waves as they break? And that was the cry of a gull as it glides overhead.

Smell

Inhale deeply through your nose and smell the unmistakable aroma of freshly baked bread.

Taste

Imagine putting a liqueur chocolate into your mouth and not chewing it, but allowing it to melt. It's got a delicious orange flavour to it, which makes your mouth water and your taste buds crave for more. Imagine having the urge to crush the chocolate with your tongue against the roof of your mouth, and the extra burst of flavour as the thick liqueur seeps out.

Touch

Feel the warm tingling sensation of the sun's caressing rays upon your face as you look upwards, closing your eyes against the brightness.

Use as many of the five senses as possible throughout your entire presentation, to trigger your customer's imagination and to create customer emotion. Then use your sixth sense, your perception, to feel your way and judge when the timing is right to close.

Step 27
Selling emotion, not logic

'Customers buy emotionally and then justify their decision with logic.' Each presentation must have a certain amount of logic. Your product must make sense, it must be financially viable. Otherwise, if a customer buys solely on emotion (on impulse), it is likely that once his emotions have cooled down he will say 'What have I done?' and he will cancel. Emotion makes the sale, logic solidifies the sale.

Every product or service is aimed at either creating a desire or satisfying a need, but people only buy on logic alone when it's a necessity, e.g. water, gas, petrol, road tax, etc. If it is not a necessity, then every purchase is made emotionally. Let me give you a couple of examples.

When you go to the supermarket for a loaf of bread (which to all intents and purposes is not a necessity), you might choose a brown sliced loaf, with added wheatgerm and extra fibre – this is an emotional purchase. You pay more to satisfy your emotional desire for the wholesome taste and the image of healthy eating.

When it's time for a new hi-fi system, instead of buying a machine that is simply capable, you spend extra money for the fully remote control with fancy buttons and switches, to satisfy your emotional desires of vanity and pride of ownership.

These are emotional sales, but now let's look at a different scenario.

Have you ever experienced the situation where the customer agrees with everything you said (the yes man) but he doesn't buy? Yes, I like it, yes, I'd use it, yes, I can see that it would save me money, yes, I can see all the benefits, yes, yes, yes, yes, yes – NO! I have to think about it. Have you ever had that? I think we all have at one time or another.

The reason this happens is because the salesperson has failed to create emotion, the customer is flat, he has no desire or need. The salesperson presented his product to the customer logically. Yes, it makes sense and the customer can see that, but nobody ever buys anything just because it makes sense. Investing in double glazing puts value on property and saves on fuel bills. This makes financial sense (in the long run), so why doesn't everybody (assuming they can afford it) buy it? Because they have no desire or need to install double glazing.

The pro-clo finds a need and creates a desire by selling benefits. Here's how he does it.

'Sell the Sizzle, Not the Sausage'

Sell the sizzle, not the sausage – in other words, sell the benefits, not the features. This will create the emotional desire or need that the customer must have to enable you to make the sale. Read that again, because it is so important.

Turn the features of your product or service into customer benefits. Practise by taking an object, any object, look at its features and then turn those features into benefits. I'll give you another example using this book, which is the only object I am aware of, for certain, that you have in front of you.

I will exaggerate to emphasize turning the features of this book into benefits. Remember that people buy benefits (emotions) not features (logic).

FEATURE: This book has a cover . . .
BENEFIT: . . . which protects the pages from becoming worn or dog-eared. The cover, which is very durable, also binds the book together and stops the pages from falling out, so your investment in this book will last many, many years.

FEATURE: There are a lot of pages . . .
BENEFIT: . . . which are full of invaluable information, techniques and tips. It is more than just a book, it is a comprehensive, easy-reading guide to success. The pages are full of proven formulas, pearls of wisdom and closing techniques that will make the reader richer in more ways than one.

FEATURE: The pages are white . . .
BENEFIT: . . . so that the print stands out boldly and is easy to see and read. The quality of the paper is such that the pages are not transparent, therefore it's possible to print on both sides.

Now, hopefully, you've got that. We take a feature and turn it into a benefit. If you haven't grasped it yet, then go back to the beginning and read through these last couple of pages again.

The next step, once you've turned a feature into a benefit, is to tie the benefit down. For example:

FEATURE: This book is very informative and also a little humorous . . .
BENEFIT: . . . which means you can enjoy learning in a light-hearted manner.

TIE-DOWN: To really take something in, it has to be repetitive and you have to enjoy it, don't you agree?

FEATURE: The apartment is set back, away from the sea front . . .
BENEFIT: . . . which means you enjoy privacy and peace and quiet but still get a magnificent view.
TIE-DOWN: That's important when choosing a holiday home, isn't it?

People buy benefits not features, they buy emotion not logic, they don't buy a product, they buy what the product will do for them. Don't sell logic (features), sell emotions and feelings (benefits).

Step 28
The emotional triggers

The pro-clo continually asks questions (his favourites are who?, what?, where?, when?, why? and how?) to find the customer's hot-button, the button that will turn the customer on and trigger the customer's emotional responses. It is these emotional triggers that will help the pro-clo close the sale.

These are the eight basic emotional triggers (there are many others that fall under the same headings):

1	PRIDE OF OWNERSHIP:	People love to own.
2	PEER PRESSURE:	Keeping up with the Joneses.
3	AMBITION:	Everyone wants to better themselves.
4	PRESTIGE AND STATUS:	People like to perceive themselves as special, they like to be noticed and they like to have status symbols to show success.
5	GREED:	One of the strongest emotions of them all.
6	FEAR OF LOSS:	Nobody wants to miss out on a good thing.
7	VANITY:	Everyone likes admiration and we all like to show off a little.
8	SECURITY:	Peace of mind is important to all of us.

Let's suppose your customer tells you that he drives a BMW with a cherished number-plate, and he collects BMW paraphernalia such as key fobs, T-shirts, ash trays, driving gloves, etc. Which emotional triggers do you suppose will switch this customer on? Certainly numbers 1, 4 and 7 above.

Now let's suppose you sell double-glazing to the same customer, which emotional triggers will you use to get the customer to buy? Right, the same ones (numbers 1, 4 and 7).

So as an example, using vanity as the emotional trigger, let's turn a feature into a benefit and tie it down.

> 'Mr Jones, the quality of our leaded windows are of the highest standard, so not only will they last you a lifetime, but they'll give you the most attractive and prestigious-looking house in the road. Just think – you'd be the envy of all the neighbours, wouldn't you?' (Raise your eyebrows and nod slightly.)

Get the idea?

Recap

Step 26   Use the senses to help create emotion, especially sight and hearing.

Step 27   Sell benefits not features, sell the sizzle not the sausage.

Step 28   Ask questions to find the customer's hot-button, his emotional trigger, and sell him that emotion.

Step 29
Tie-downs

In his book and audio programme *How to Master the Art of Selling Anything*, the American sales trainer Tom

Hopkins demonstrates that he is a true 'champion' in the use of tie-downs. This next step I accredit to his teachings.

The 'tie-down' is a question asked at the end of a statement to obtain a minor yes, or a positive response. The more yes's and positive responses a pro-clo gets throughout his presentation, the more likely the end result will be the positive response – the ultimate YES!

'Tie-downs' are also great for keeping the customers involved in the presentation. He can't just sit back and listen – *(can he?)*, he has to get involved – *(doesn't he?)*. The more involved he becomes, and the more positive responses you get, the more likely you are to achieve the sale – *(aren't you?)*.

I have listed below some important 'tie-downs'. The more you use and practise them, the more natural they will become and the more sales you will close. That's what we're all after – *(isn't it?)*.

wasn't it	couldn't it	shouldn't it
wouldn't it	don't you agree	wouldn't you agree
wouldn't they	didn't you	didn't they
won't you	won't they	won't we
couldn't you	couldn't they	couldn't we
hasn't he	hasn't she	haven't they
aren't they	aren't we	isn't it
isn't that right	doesn't it	weren't they
weren't we	shouldn't they	shouldn't we

Inverted Tie-Downs

Instead of asking a question at the end of a statement, e.g. 'Our computerized planning of your kitchen makes optimum use of space, don't you agree?', we ask a question at the beginning of the statement to come across more softly, with a friendlier approach: 'Don't you agree that our computerized planning of your kitchen makes optimum use of space?'

Try this exercise and see if you can 'tie down' the following statements.

> We can do it . . .
> It would be good . . .
> They were brilliant . . .
> It is nice . . .
> They should do it . . .
> They are right . . .
> We are the best . . .
> Now I'm getting there . . .
> See, I can do this . . .
> I have cracked it now . . . YES!

And so you have, but now you've cracked this little technique, it is important to understand that using too many tie-downs or using them too frequently becomes very irritating, doesn't it? You're following me, aren't you? I'm sure you understand, don't you?, and I know you will agree, won't you?

A pro-clo doesn't over-use tie-downs. Instead he only ties down statements that are of consequence, and he always sounds natural.

Step 30
Creating urgency

The most effective way to create the necessary environment for people to buy is to create urgency.

Once the customer has an interest or desire in the product, the pro-clo will subject him to a feeling of fear (fear of losing out) by creating urgency.

It is important to understand that urgency will only be effective if there is a desire for the product. Remember, you can only close a door that has been opened.

The most effective ways to create urgency are:

1   *Take-away*
    We will be looking at how this classic works in the next step (31).

2   *Special offer*
    Make your customer a special offer, one that is tailor-made just for him.

3   *Limited availability*
    It's 'only while stocks last' so the customer had better get one while he can.

4   *Limited period*
    The offer ends on Saturday so the customer must get on board now, otherwise he will miss the boat.

5   *Additional discount*
    As an incentive if you take the order today. (Justified because you save your company time and money if you don't have to call back.)

6   *Imminent price increase*
    The customer should get in while the going is good.

7   *The auction-like atmosphere of the sales office/
    showroom*
    They're going like hot cakes. That customer over there
    has just bought one, and that one over there.

8   *Create a waiting list*
    There's a six-week waiting list for these particular
    units so the customer had better order some more
    right now.

9   *Have a sale*
    Everyone has an eye for a bargain. This product has
    20 per cent off today or 10 per cent off tomorrow!

10 *Say it's sold*
    'Mr Jones, I'm sorry, I've just been told that one is
    sold . . . but if I could get you another one . . .'

When creating this 'sense of urgency', if the pro-clo is
not sincere or convincing, the customer will see it as a sales
gimmick, and the urgency will be lost and, most probably,
so will the sale. Each and every customer, to some degree,
must be subjected to this 'sense of urgency' – it creates the
pressure needed to make the customer do it now.

Understand that even when the customer is completely
sold, most of the time he doesn't want to buy right now,
at this very moment. The customer, if he were given the
chance, would much rather have time to reflect or would
rather do the paperwork some other time, when it's more
convenient.

The urgency, or fear, is just another piece of the jigsaw
puzzle that the pro-clo slots into place at the right time.

Step 31
Take-aways

A pro-clo knows that his customers want what they can't have. Paul Stewart, whom I quoted earlier (p.102), puts it more eloquently:

> The forbidden fruit is always thought to be sweeter. In other words, the item that we know we can't have is often the most desirable and enjoyable to attain.

The pro-clo is such a tease, he deliberately tells a customer that they can't have something or it's not available, to increase the customer's desire. It is important to remember that you have to create a certain amount of interest before you can 'take it away'. It would be pointless to tell somebody they can't have something when they have no desire for it whatsoever.

Create an interest, implement a take-away, and you'll end up with a desire.

Consider this analogy.

> A small child is walking by and as he does so you stop him, take a toffee lollipop out of your pocket and ask the child if he would like to have it. The little boy's eyes light up, he nods his head and goes to take the lollipop, but as he does so, you pull it away and say: 'Ha, ha, only joking.' The child's expression turns to one of frustration and disappointment, so you offer it to him again. The child perks up, he sees that you were only teasing so he tries to take the lollipop again – as he does so you pull it away. The more this happens, the more the child wants

the lollipop. What started as a fleeting whim turns into a burning desire, so much so that the child starts to stamp his feet and yell.

Create an interest, implement a take-away, you'll end up with a desire.

It is very important that the take-away sounds genuine, otherwise the customer will see straight through it. It is also very important not to overdo it, otherwise when you give the customer what he wants you will lose credibility – the customer will see that you have tried to trick him and he won't buy.

The hardest thing for a salesperson to say to a customer is 'No'. No it's not available, no, that option is not open to you, no, I can't do that, no, I won't do that, no, no, no, no, no!

Customers expect all salespeople to say 'Yes'. Yes, it will do this, yes, it will do that, yes, I can do that for you, and so on. If you say 'No' occasionally, not only will you become more trustworthy in the customer's eyes, but you will in effect implement a take-away. Besides, if you say no to something, you can always change your mind, back down and give in to the customer – let him feel he has accomplished something. On the other hand, if you have said yes, you can hardly then change your mind and expect the customer to still purchase.

Let me give you an example.

CUSTOMER: 'I'd want a discount for cash.'
SALESPERSON: 'OK, I'll give you 2½ per cent for paying cash.'

Here, the salesperson gains nothing. He has agreed with the customer (sympathy instead of empathy). He hasn't closed the customer, instead he waits to see if the customer will buy. The customer might think the salesperson gave in too easily, there must be a catch, maybe it's overpriced, if I hold out I might get more discount, and so the customer says 'I'll think about it and let you know.'

Now, instead of saying yes, let's say no. Same example.

CUSTOMER: 'I'd want a discount for cash.'

PRO-CLO: 'I'm sorry, Mr Jones, we work on fixed prices. I'm not able to take anything off.'

Now the customer will either give in or object. If he gives in, the pro-clo makes more commission. But let's say he objects.

CUSTOMER: 'Well, if I don't get a discount, I'm not buying.'

PRO-CLO: 'Mr Jones, I don't know if I could do this, but it's worth a try . . . if I can clear it through head office to give you a 2 per cent quantity discount, on the proviso you take immediate delivery, can I have your order today?'

Remember, sound genuine and don't overdo it.

The take-away, and saying 'No', are great closing tools.

Step 32
Trial closing

Throughout the entire presentation, the pro-clo is continually testing the water to get positive responses from
the customer. The pro-clo doesn't necessarily complete his
entire presentation before attempting to close because he
knows that frequently the customer is ready to buy before
he has heard everything. (This is referred to as 'timing',
which is the technique we shall be looking at next.)

There are some salespeople who insist on completing
their presentation and giving the customer every piece of
information before allowing the customer to buy – often
these salespeople will go past the close, they in effect
oversell. If you keep talking when the customer is ready to
buy, the customer is more likely to come up with objections
and say something like 'Oh, I didn't think of that'.

As soon as the pro-clo feels the customer is ready to
purchase, he will test the water with a trial close – seeking
a positive response. If the response is forthcoming, the
pro-clo will immediately attempt to close the sale.

At the beginning of the presentation, the pro-clo tests
the water with involvement questions: 'How would you
use this?' or 'Where would you install one?' or 'What
would you do first?', and so on. Then, as the presentation gets under way and the customer's responses are
more positive, the trial closing takes on a more direct
approach: 'Do you prefer red or blue?' or 'We deliver
on Tuesdays or Fridays, which is the more convenient
for you?' or 'Do you want two or three?'. If the customer
responds positively to these trial closes, it shows a willing-
ness to buy – and it's time to close.

If the customer responds negatively to a trial close,

for instance 'I don't want it in red *or* blue' or 'I didn't say I was buying, so delivery dates are irrelevant', all it means is that the customer is not ready yet. In this case, the pro-clo would respond by saying 'I'm sorry, I didn't mean to decide for you', then he would simply carry on with the presentation as if nothing had happened.

Step 33
Timing

Throughout the presentation, the pro-clo keeps his eyes open for an opportunity to close. He waits until the timing is just right, and then he strikes – while the iron is hot.

If you attempt to close too early, the customer will see it as being arrogant and pushy. This will make the sale very difficult, if not impossible, to close. On the other hand, if you leave it too late you will go past the close, you will oversell, which will definitely lose the sale.

A pro-clo waits until the timing is right before he attempts to close. When he feels the customer has been fed enough information and owner benefits, when he feels the customer understands enough about the product to be able to make the buying decision, the pro-clo goes in to close.

It is comparable to bending an iron bar. If you heat it up until it is warm and then try bending it, it will resist your attempts, and will either cool down rapidly or snap with the pressure. If you heat the iron bar too much it loses shape, it becomes distorted and turns into liquid. (The customer gets oversold, he thinks there's a catch, so he runs away.) Only when the iron bar is red-hot does it bend easily and willingly.

A pro-clo waits until his customer is hot, then when the
timing is right he strikes and the customer gives way easily
and willingly. There are many signs or buying signals which
tell the pro-clo that the time is right to ask the customer
for the order. Below are some of the most common buying
signals. Watch out for them.

It's time to close when the customer:

1   Looks at his spouse/colleague with raised eyebrows.
2   Nibbles or bites at his lip.
3   Scratches his head whilst looking downwards.
4   Nods in agreement with what you are saying.
5   The pupil (of the eye) dilates showing approval.
6   Rubs his chin or the back of his head.
7   Begins tapping his fingers.
8   Stares out of the window with a thoughtful expression.
9   Strokes his beard or pulls at his moustache.
10 Smiles contentedly.
11 Leans forward, interested.
12 Asks 'what if' questions – 'What if . . . ?'
13 Becomes still, especially a fidgeting foot.
14 Picks up or handles the sales material.
15 Licks his lips.
16 Continuously strokes his hair.
17 Continuously looks from the sales material to the
    closer and back again.
18 Asks a question about something that has already been
    covered – 'Can you go over that again?'
19 Repeats a question he has already asked.
20 Moves his lips silently as if reckoning up.

There are many more buying signals. The important
thing to remember is, don't close too early or too late
– wait until you feel the customer has taken in enough
product knowledge and owner benefits to make a decision.

Then be aware of your timing – use one or two trial closes and watch the body language for buying signals.

Recap

Step 29 Use 'tie-downs' to involve and close your customer, but don't over-use them.

Step 30 Create the necessary environment to close the sale by creating urgency.

Step 31 Create an interest, implement a 'take-away', and you'll end up with a desire.

Step 32 Test the water with trial closes.

Step 33 Strike while the iron is hot. Watch for the customer's buying signals.

Step 34
Recap before going in

Before you actually ask your customer for the order, it is a good idea to go over the owner benefits again, to make sure the customer understands everything, to make sure there are no last-minute doubts or questions, to make sure that all of the benefits are in the forefront of the customer's mind when you ask him to buy.

Don't bore him with the whole presentation again, just briefly summarize the major facts that will help persuade the customer to purchase. It is impossible for the customer to remember everything he has seen and heard, so this quick recap (lasting maybe 20 seconds) is to re-educate him and to confirm that value has been established.

As we discussed earlier, first we tell them what we are going to do (setting the stage), then we do it (kiss and tell, the presentation) and finally we tell them what we've just done (recap owner benefits) before we ask for the commitment.

Step 35
If you don't ask, you don't get

Waiting for a customer to buy (especially in direct sales) is like waiting for the cows to come home. The customer has to be asked to buy, because if you don't ask, you don't get – it's as simple as that.

There are so many salespeople out there who fail because they are frightened to ask the customer for the order. Some of these so-called salespeople do an excellent job in selling the customer, but then they don't ask for the order, they don't close. They do all the groundwork and then give up – they are, in effect, working for the competition, because rest assured, if the customer *is* convinced the competition will ask him to buy and the customer will end up buying from them.

Whilst training recruits and existing salespeople to become professional closers, I've met thousands of people with this same problem. They know how to sell but they don't know how to close – instead, they wait for the customer to buy. Their repertoire of actual closes normally consists of only one or two, which go something like this: 'Well . . . what do you think?' or 'How about it?' The customer's typical response to this feeble attempt is to say: 'Everything looks great, if you leave it with me, I'll mull it over and I'm pretty sure we'll do business.' I know it's difficult to believe, but these salespeople actually get excited when their customers say this to them. The customer ends up selling the salesperson – who does exactly what he is asked, for instance: 'That's great, Mr Jones, I'll leave you these brochures and my card and I'll get back to you in a couple of days. How does that sound?'

If the above passage sounds all too familiar, don't worry, we've all been there. By the time you finish this book you will not only find closing easy but also lots of fun. Read on.

FACT: Only 3 per cent of customers (direct selling) actually offer to buy, saying something like 'That sounds good to me, I'll take it', or 'OK, I'm happy, let's do it', or 'You've just got yourself a deal'. The remaining 97 per cent have to be asked to buy and to buy today!

If you sell but don't ask for the order or close the sale – instead you wait for the customer to buy – your closing percentage will only ever be 3 per cent – which means you won't be in the profession for very long.

When the timing is right, ask the customer for the order and ask confidently – don't mumble, or spit it out as fast as you can to get it over with.

Below are a few examples of asking for the order. You will find more in Part Three on page 230.

'If I can find you the right one, are you prepared to go ahead today?'

'If I could get that particular unit for you right now, would you have it?'

'If I could get approval on that, are you willing to take it today?'

'If I could make this comfortable for you, financially, you'd have one right now, wouldn't you?'

'If the money side of this is OK – will you join us today?'

'Aside from the money, would there be anything else that would stop you from taking advantage of this, right now?'

Don't try to be someone else, ask them in your own words – just let go. The important thing is to ASK, and if they should say no or object, use another close, then ASK again and again and again . . .

In the beginning it always feels a little awkward, but the more you practise, the better you will become and the more natural you will sound.

Now, on to the next technique, which is just as important.

Step 36
The pressure of silence

This next technique is one of the most widely known rules in our profession and yet it is a rule that is frequently broken. The rule is, *once you ask the customer for the order, you SHUT UP*, you stay silent for as long as it takes for the customer to respond.

From experience, I've found that the longer the silence, the more likely it is that the customer will say yes. But let me tell you, those silent seconds feel like minutes, and when the silence runs into a few minutes, the pressure to speak makes it feel like hours.

The pressure that this silence causes is felt by both the customer and the salesperson, but the actual pressure to speak, to break the silence, is felt much more by the salesperson.

The reason the rule is frequently broken is that the salesperson can't handle this pressure, he can't bear the silence, he has to speak. His voice is bouncing around his head looking for a way out, and so the salesperson speaks, he gives in and starts blabbering on again.

The pro-clo feels the same way, he also feels the pressure to break the silence, but he resists this pressure and his lips remain sealed. The pro-clo will not speak first, he will not break the customer's train of thought, because he knows that during this silent interlude the customer is thinking to himself: 'Well, shall I do it or not? – I'd certainly love to have it and everything looks to be in order – supposing I was to go ahead, then – I'm sure that I can manage the payments, besides, if I ever did get into difficulty, I could always sell it again – I wonder what John and Mary will say – yeah, I reckon so . . .'

Psychologically, the first person to break the silence is the first person to give in. Obviously a pro-clo doesn't want to give in (without first putting up a fight), so ask the question and then let the customer be the next person to speak.

For the best results, follow this procedure.

1   Ask the customer to 'give it a try'.

2   Sit back in your chair and remain silent.

3   For extra pressure, lean slightly forward and hold out
    your hand.

4   Keep your gaze fixed firmly on the customer's eyes.
    He will not maintain eye contact until he is ready to
    speak. Instead, he will probably keep glancing at the
    table and the papers.

5   Maintain a slight, confident and friendly smile whilst
    you watch and wait for your customer.

6   Send out positive vibes – say to yourself over and over
    'Go on, buy it, buy it, buy it . . .' And guess what?
    They will, they will, they will!

Remember, the longer the silence, the better the chances
of a sale – because it means the customer can't think of a
reason not to buy. Don't be tempted to break the silence.
Bite your tongue, until it bleeds if necessary.

Recap

Step 34 Re-educate the customer with a brief recap of
         the owner benefits before closing.

Step 35 Ask for the order.

Step 36 Don't say another word until the customer
         responds.

Step 37
Be-backs are a myth

Tomorrow is a promissory note,
Yesterday is an IOU,
Today is cash at the bank.
(*Anon.*)

A pro-clo doesn't believe in 'call-backs' or 'be-backs'
– he knows that if the customer calls or comes back
to buy, he should have been closed on the day. In all
but the very isolated cases (maybe 1 in 1,000), the fact
that the customer didn't buy there and then is simply
down to the fact that the closer gave up, he got weak
on himself (probably because he became too close to
his customer and didn't want to offend him by closing the sale), he didn't persist.

In every single sales presentation, someone gets sold
– either the closer sells the customer or the customer
sells the closer. Even a pro-clo – who doesn't believe in
be-backs (he knows they don't exist) – still gets caught
out occasionally, e.g.: 'This is the one, this guy is genuine,
you'll see, this will be the 1 in 1,000. This customer is
going to buy, he'll call back first thing tomorrow morning, I know it, I feel it!' Here, the pro-clo has been
so well sold (by the customer) that he justifies his own
belief.

Understand that 99 times out of 100, when a customer
says 'I'll be back' or 'I'll get back to you' he sincerely
means it. The customer is sold, the customer wants the
product, he has a desire and need for it, the customer
feels obligated because he used up so much of the salesperson's time. He wants to buy, but he doesn't want to

buy right now, not in the euphoria of the moment. The customer wants to sit back and reflect, to be absolutely sure. So when a customer says 'I'll be back', most of the time he sincerely means it.

Question
If the customer is so sincere, then what happens? Why doesn't he come back, or call back, to buy?

Answer
Remember, when the customer is most excited and enthused about a product is when he is easiest to close. When the customer leaves the sales environment, he starts to come down again, to become his old logical self. Once the logic sets in, the customer says to himself (to ease his conscience) 'I'll do it next year', or 'I'll wait until after Christmas'. In essence, the customer thinks of every reason not to buy rather than, when he was with the salesperson, every reason to go ahead.

Out of sight is out of mind. If you let the customer go, he will forget most of what he has been told.

As I said earlier, in every presentation someone gets sold. The pro-clo does not and will not believe in be-backs. He knows that a verbal contract is not worth the paper it's written on. (This topic will be covered again in Part 2, objection no. 8.)

If the pro-clo gets too close to his customer, it can be tough to close the sale – but when the going gets tough, the tough get going and the weak give in. Don't ever give in, go for it! It's better to get a 'no', than a 'maybe'. At least with a 'no' you can forget about it and concentrate on the next one.

Step 38
Handling failure (without the doom and gloom)

Although this next step is important to all salespeople everywhere, it is particularly pertinent to those involved in direct sales or commission only sales, for they are the ones who succeed through failing the most.

In our industry, the price of success is failure. In fact, there is only one industry in the entire world where ratios of failure, sometimes well over 50 per cent, can still guarantee outstanding success – the sales industry.

A professional closer, the best of the best, will fail most of the time – and yet he is deemed an expert, a professional, a leader in his field, and a master of success and achievement. The pro-clo who fails more times than he succeeds still makes more money than any other professional and also has job security for life. Imagine, for a second, a doctor or a solicitor failing more than 50 per cent of the time! They wouldn't remain in their profession for very long, would they?

The first rule of handling failure is to accept that it is inevitable. Ours is a numbers game. In direct sales, especially, you have to see so many people to make a sale, maybe one in four. The trouble is that you don't know which is the one, so you have to give 100 per cent effort to all four in order to achieve a sale.

(*Note:* if you're dealing with warm leads, maybe existing owners, owner referrals, or customers who come to you with an interest, your failure rate may be as low as 10 per cent – in other words, you may *succeed* 90 per cent of the time. However, we are not talking about that here, because in these instances you don't need to handle failure, as such.)

A pro-clo knows the dishonour is not in falling down but in staying down. He knows that if at first you don't succeed, you must try, try and try again. Nobody ever pretends it is easy, because it most definitely is not, and every professional occasionally gets on a downer. It is impossible to stay up every minute of every day for every week in every year – the key is to learn how to handle and accept failure and not stay down. Remember what I said at the beginning of this book: 'Selling can be the best-paid, hardest job in the world or the worst-paid, easiest job in the world.' The choice is yours!

Although ours is a numbers game, there can be a certain amount of luck involved. You see, luck tends to come to those positive individuals who look for it, expecting to find it. However, luck doesn't come into it over a prolonged period of time, and that's one of the ways of handling failure – looking at things over a period of time, rather than in the heat of the moment. The professional knows that there are going to be ups and downs. He knows that sometimes he won't be able to put a foot wrong, every customer will buy, and his monthly closing percentage will soar. The next minute, the complete opposite may occur, and the pro-clo can't do anything right. Then he fights it tooth and nail until he succeeds again. The pro-clo learns to ride the wave through the peaks and the troughs.

There is only one good way to avoid failing – never try. Assuming that you don't heed the above sentence, understand and accept that failure is the road to success. Fight failure with all your heart and you will succeed in conquering some of the defeats, but when you feel down, as you sometimes will (if you're human), follow the steps outlined below to handle failure successfully.

1   If you make a mistake that costs you a sale, then by all means feel angry with yourself and learn from that mistake, but don't make the mistake of feeling sorry for yourself. Continued success or failure is not an immediate thing, but something that evolves over a period of time. A pro-clo looks at failure in the wider perspective – over the course of six months or a year his closing percentages may or may not increase, but they don't fall, so how can he be failing?

2   Understand that it is better to have tried and failed than not to have tried at all. Look for some good in every failure – if you look hard enough, you'll succeed in finding it.

3   After each failure, subject yourself to a complete self-analysis, treat each disappointment as an opportunity to learn from your mistakes, and concentrate on perfecting your performance.

4   When you're feeling down, say positive statements with emotion and conviction over and over, and force positive thoughts into your subconscious. Change your thinking patterns and attitude from negative to positive again.

5   Obviously prevention is better than cure, and the best medicine to shake off the oncoming clouds of doom and despair is to do what only a pro-clo is capable of doing: get up, dust yourself off, and go get yourself a deal.

Understand that if there were no such thing as failure, there would be no such thing as success. Accept that you will fail – it's all part of the job – but that's not to say you shouldn't dig your heels in and fight it every step of the way.

Step 39
The difference between being good and being the best

This last technique in this section is probably the most widely known success technique there is, and yet it is the most ignored. Salespeople fight this technique. They don't use it because they don't grasp the importance of it. They ignore it, or can't be bothered, or put it off until tomorrow, or next week or the new year, but until whenever never comes.

This technique is what makes the difference between being good and earning good rewards, or being the best and continually striving forwards, getting better and better all the time. In every walk of life there are failures, there are poor performers, there are those who accept mediocrity, then there are those who are competent and good – finally, there's that rare breed, the outstanding achievers, the professionals. I've met some good closers in my time, but the best of the best always have something in common, they use the technique that everyone else ignores or says 'Not that old rubbish again!'.

The technique is goal-setting. The mark of the pro-clo (or those who aspire to be) is that he or she has goals – clearly defined, written-down goals.

I can remember fighting this technique, so I know why so many people fail to use it. I used to think that goals were dreams and wishful thinking. I used to think that what is important is today, not tomorrow. I knew lots of losers who supposedly had goals and failed to achieve them, and I was forever hearing the also-rans saying things like 'I wish I had his luck' or 'I'd like a Porsche' or 'Wouldn't it be great to be rich!'. I considered myself to be pretty good without all these dreams and wishful thoughts – I had the attitude of 'I'm doing fine just as I am, thank you very much!'.

I bumped into using the technique of goal-setting quite by accident whilst striving to meet a sales bonus, a fairly handsome reward, but on the very distant horizon. I remember breaking down on paper exactly how much business I would have to write, how many customers I would have to convert on a monthly basis, a weekly basis and a daily basis to get that sales bonus. I knew that if one day I failed to meet my target, the next day I would have to work twice as hard. This was a goal that someone else had set for me, a challenge – and when I achieved it by monitoring my performance . . . well, let me tell you, it felt pretty good!

After that success, I learned and read everything I could on the art of goal-setting . Then I adapted my knowledge to fit not only my career but my entire life.

Goal-setting *is* important and anybody who does it, I mean really does it, will tell you so. The only problem is there are so few people who actually do it. If you haven't until now, then at least give it a try – what harm can it do? Use these simple, easy-to-follow rules.

1   Always write your goals down on paper, because it increases clarity and allows you to review them. Only when goals are written down do they have any substance. If they're not written down, they're a dream. When you write down your goals, KISS it (keep it short and simple). You need to be able to read or

see your goals at a glance, so don't write pages upon pages of literature – one or two lines is ample.

2   Goals must be passionately desired, otherwise you won't stretch for them. If you wouldn't mind owning a speed boat or you quite fancy the idea of a bigger house, or it would be great to be wealthy, then you'll never get there. A goal should be something that you would really like to have, in other words, I WANT IT!

3   Your written goals should be specific, like in the example I gave on breaking down what I had to do and when I had to do it by, to get that sales bonus. It is no good writing 'I want to earn a lot of money', or 'I want to be rich', because that just isn't specific enough. It's no good writing 'I want to earn £100,000' because that isn't specific enough either. You have to decide when you want it by. For example:

I WANT TO EARN £100,000 IN THE NEXT 12 MONTHS
To achieve this goal, I need to earn £8,333 per month, which is £1,923 per week.
My average order value is £1,940 – my commission is 10 per cent so I earn on average £194 per sale.
To achieve this goal I need to make ten sales a week, which is two sales a day.

Now, that's specific, but is it realistic?

4   Be realistic, otherwise you're dreaming again. It would not be realistic to say 'I want to make £1 million this week'. (If it were, I doubt very much if you would be

reading this book.) You must believe that a goal is achievable, otherwise you won't work for it. A goal should not be too easy or too difficult, but it should make sure that you work hard to obtain it.

5 You must monitor your activity towards your goals, you must be aware of how you're doing so that you can inspire yourself to greater performance.

6 You should frequently review and regularly update your goals. If things are running ahead of target, don't relax or sit back. Instead, increase the goal to demand higher but achievable performance. On the other hand, if things are running way behind schedule and it looks as though you have no chance of reaching your goal – don't give up and say that goal-setting doesn't work, just because you were a little over-optimistic. (Optimism is a good thing, so don't let it turn into pessimism.) Instead, review and update the goal, make it more realistic, and then concentrate on smashing through it.

7 Keep your goals *your goals*, keep them private. Don't allow others to have the opportunity of trying to pull you down or discourage you. The people who do this kind of thing, and there are many of them, do so because they feel overshadowed by your enthusiasm and threatened by your success. They don't want to accept that you are better than them. As we discussed earlier in this book, a pro-clo often works alone and is somewhat possessive. This isn't to say that he isn't liked, or that he isn't generous and helpful to his colleagues – in fact, he is the complete opposite with other eager and positive individuals – but he does keep himself and his goals to himself. Even when a pro-clo

achieves a goal, he keeps it to himself. He doesn't brag or show off to make others envious. Rather he smiles, bends his head whilst raising his arm with a clenched fist, and he says to himself in capital letters: 'YEAH'. Then he sets another goal to replace the one he has just lost, by winning it.

8   Finally, you should make four types of goal.
   (a) Long-term goals – goals for the next 5, 10, 15 years ahead. A pro-clo always knows where he is going. Although long-term goal planning is important, you should not pay too much importance to specifics. The farther away something is, the less important it seems. The general idea here is to have specific targets to aim for.
   (b) Medium-term goals – goals ranging from 12 to 60 months. These are the goals that you really desire the most now, e.g. the boat, the car, the promotion, etc. Review and update these goals the most.
   (c) Short-term goals – goals ranging from 1 to 12 months. These are the mile markers to the marathon runner, the goals that create the inspiration to motor on. They are the goals where success and rewards are right around the next corner, so you steam ahead in anticipation.
   (d) Immediate-term goals – ranging from 1 to 30 days. For me, these are the best. These are the goals that we set each day, each week, the ones that give us a continuous sense of happiness and accomplishment as we succeed in our endeavours.

Summary

1 Always write your goals down.

2 Make sure that you genuinely desire your goals.

3 Be specific on how to achieve them and by when.

4 Be realistic but optimistic.

5 Monitor your activity towards your goals.

6 Review and update them regularly.

7 Keep them to yourself.

8 Set different-range goals, especially immediate-term.

I'm going to finish off this section by repeating something I wrote earlier. Read it again, and digest it.

Set yourself achievable goals. It is important to have something to strive for, otherwise you will end up wandering around without a destination – like a piece of driftwood aimlessly bobbing up and down on the ocean. A person becomes stale when his dreams equal his present being. He lacks desire and ambition and ends up existing instead of thriving. A professional closer sets himself goals, and as he nears or attains them, he sets himself new desires, new goals, and off he goes again, never ending, always thriving.

Start planning straight away – it feels so much better when you have a route to follow.

Quote
>   Where there is no vision, the people perish.
>   (*Holy Bible, Proverbs 29: 18*)

Visualize your success, plan your route and set your goals.

GO FOR IT!

PART TWO

Overcoming Objections

Objections

What Is an Objection?

An objection is a statement of interest, a veiled request for more information. Let me explain.

A customer objects because something concerns him – but he wouldn't be concerned unless he was interested, would he? So an objection is a statement that shows the customer is interested but needs more information.

Before we get into this subject of objections, it is important to understand what is *not* an objection!

When a customer is asked to purchase, if he doesn't agree immediately he will respond with an objection – or he will respond with a condition, an excuse, or a flat no. Let's look at these responses.

1   *The Condition*
    A condition is a genuine reason that stops the customer from going ahead (normally lack of money). The customer is sold right down the line and if it weren't for the condition, he would have purchased. This is nobody's fault, and if it's not possible to implement a compromise the pro-clo will move on taking comfort from the fact that he has done his job as best he could.

2   *The Excuse (The Leak)*
    Here, the customer makes up an excuse to get him
    off the hook. In this situation, the customer is not
    sold on the product (or maybe the company), but
    he does, however, feel some obligation towards the
    salesperson. The customer has used up a lot of
    the salesperson's time and so he feels somewhat
    awkward, but still, he's not sold and he's not going
    to buy. The customer comes up with an excuse
    so that he doesn't hurt the salesperson's feelings.
    For example, the customer might say: 'Well, every-
    thing seems fine but I just need to sleep on it
    tonight, and go over a few things in my mind.
    What time do you open in the morning?' Here,
    the salesperson has got his work cut out, but with
    persistence the sale can be closed.

3   *The Flat No (The Potato)*
    The customer declines to go ahead, he is simply not
    sold and so he refuses to purchase. It could be that
    the customer is not sold on the salesperson or that he
    is not sold on the product or even the company.
    In any event, this not sold response is the sales-
    person's fault – he has failed in his job because he
    hasn't been effective. In this situation it will obvi-
    ously be very difficult, if not impossible, to close the
    sale.

An objection, however, means something completely
different. When a customer states an objection, it means
that he is too committed to say 'No, I don't want it'.
When a customer states an objection it means that he
has a desire or a need for the product, but he is not yet
entirely convinced. When a customer states an objection
it means he is frightened or sceptical or cautious.

The two most important things to remember whenever you hear an objection are (a) the customer is too committed to say 'No' and (b) the customer has a desire for the product. Armed with these two pieces of ammunition, every objection can be overcome.

An objection, translated, means 'OK, I'm committed, I can't say that I don't want it because I do, but I'm just not sure if it's the right thing to do, I need more information, I need more convincing, otherwise I'm not going to buy'. A customer's doubt or concern is expressed as an objection, a need for more information.

In a moment we are going to look at a few common objections and I will show you how to read between the lines and translate them. Then I will explain some general rules and principles about objections so that you know what to do and what not to do. Later in this section I will give you the Six-Step Formula to overcome an objection before, finally, taking forty-two of the most common objections and giving you the means to counter each of them and turn them into a close.

Overcoming Objections

First let's read between the lines and decipher what the customer is actually saying.

OBJECTION	TRANSLATION
It costs too much.	I'm sold, I want one but I don't want to pay that much for it. It's not that I can't afford it, it's just more than I want to pay – I need more information to justify buying it.

I want to think about it.	I like it and I'm tempted but I feel unsure and a little scared. I'd like some time to think of reasons not to buy – I need more convincing, I need more information.
I want to compare it with others.	OK, I'm sold, I want one, but I want to be sure I buy the best one, I want to see what the competition has to offer – I need more convincing, I need more information.
I want to speak to my accountant, bank manager, granny, dog.	I'm interested, I'm almost there, but I'd much rather slow things down and get some reassurance from whoever – I need more convincing, I need more information.
I can't afford it.	I like it but I don't want one badly enough to part with my money. (If anyone wants something, really wants something, he will find a way to afford it.) Sell me some more – I need more information.

When you read between the lines, every objection is simply a request for more information. In 99.9 per cent of all cases, the only real objection is the money – after all, if your product were free, every customer would have one, wouldn't they? Nobody would ever want to think about it, or speak to their accountant, or compare it with others, if it were free – they would all have one. So the only real reason to stop them going ahead is always money.

One more time, *an objection is a statement of interest, a veiled request for more information.* Put another way, an objection means the benefits of your product are not yet worth enough for the customer to part with his money.

A pro-clo rarely receives objections when actually closing the sale, because he anticipates them throughout his presentation and eliminates the possibility of their occurring at the end. A pro-clo is like a soldier on an assault course, he knows there are obstacles that must be overcome, he knows that timing and technique are important, and he knows that he must have stamina and positive mental attitude to reach the finishing line before he runs out of steam. To a soldier it's just a matter of fitness. To a pro-clo it's just a matter of knowledge.

A pro-clo expects to receive objections – they show that he has done a good job. The customer is involved and is thinking about owning the product but voices an objection, a concern, and the pro-clo has the knowledge, the stamina and the techniques to overcome the objection and head off towards the finishing line.

Creating an Objection

Ludicrous as this may sound to a novice, to a professional closer, this is one of the easiest ways of closing the sale. Allow me to explain.

You've just completed a smooth, easy-flowing presentation and it went down well, except the customer wasn't as involved as you would have liked him to have been and you haven't heard any objections. You know that the customer is interested but yet your perception tells you that the customer is not ready to buy. What do you do? . . . You give the customer an objection to grab hold of. Give him an excuse, an escape hatch, and watch him grasp it and hold on, with both hands. To illustrate, here are some examples.

'Mr Jones, I'm fairly certain that the only thing that would stop you from going ahead right now is the initial deposit, isn't that right?'

'Mr Jones, am I right in assuming that the only thing that would stop you from giving us your order is your concern about our delivery schedule?'

'Mr Jones, if it wasn't for the fact that you're concerned about tying up all of your savings, you'd put everything into this investment plan, wouldn't you?'

It is obviously very important that you are able to overcome any objections you create. There are three golden rules to follow when creating an objection for the customer.

1   Only create an objection you can convincingly overcome.

2   Always tie the objection down – get the customer to agree that this is what is stopping him from going ahead.

3   Overcome the objection to the customer's satisfaction, then ask for the order.

Minor Objections

All customers have an in-built defence mechanism that causes reflex actions when threatened. These reflex actions are mostly minor objections which should be completely ignored. When a customer states a minor objection, the objection is not a real one, it is stated in a reflex action, without thought, to throw the salesperson off balance. A pro-clo doesn't even acknowledge these minor objections, he just continues as if he hasn't heard them.

Consider this scenario.

A customer walks into a clothes shop. No sooner is she through the door than an assistant asks 'Can I help you?'. The customer immediately feels threatened and her in-built defence mechanism causes a reflex action, so without thought she states a minor objection: 'No thanks, I'm just looking.'

The shop assistant usually falls at the first hurdle, by acknowledging and accepting the objection – but a pro-clo would ignore this minor objection and continue: 'That's fine, madam, please feel free to browse around. If you need me for anything, I'll be over there. By the way was there anything in particular you were looking for?' If the pro-clo were to get a nonchalant response, he might then make a suggestion, e.g. 'You might be interested to know that we have a special sale on these items'.

All minor objections should be completely ignored, they are simply reflex actions. If you hear a loud noise and you are not prepared for it, you become startled, your reflex action is to jump. If a customer feels threatened or is asked to buy before he is prepared, his reflex action is to state a minor objection. *Ignore it.*

Never Argue with an Objection

When a customer gives an objection, the human tendency is to argue with it, to prove that you're right and he's wrong, to beat the customer into submission. If you argue with a customer you may win the battle (prove your point) but you will always lose the war (lose the sale).

Never, ever, argue with a customer.

Imagine what would happen when the customer comes out with the objection 'It costs too much' if the salesperson argued and said 'What do you mean, it costs too much? It doesn't cost much at all, I'll have you know, blah, blah, blah . . .' Not wanting to labour the point, DON'T ARGUE, resist the temptation. It is worth mentioning that some of the best salespeople are diplomats and politicians – they don't argue, they debate, and always have a convincing answer. (At least, good ones do.)

Ignore First-Time Objections

As a general rule of thumb, always ignore the objection the first time it is given, just continue as if nothing has happened, and you will be surprised how many times the objection is forgotten about. If you ignore the objection the first time it is stated the customer will respond in one of three ways. He will either (a) forget about it, (b) answer his own objection, or (c) repeat the objection.

Isolate the Objection

When a customer states an objection you should isolate it – find out if there is any other reason for not going ahead.

If you don't isolate the objection, then as soon as you have answered it, the customer might come up with another objection, then another and another. Isolating objections does not guarantee that other objections won't come up but it does minimize the chances.

Aside from the (*objection*) would there be anything else stopping you from going ahead?'
'Apart from . . .'
'Other than . . .'
'Is that the only thing stopping you?'

Empathy

Always respond to an objection with empathy, never sympathy.

Empathy = I understand how you feel. But . . .
= I appreciate what you are saying. However . . .
= I agree with that. But what if . . . ?
= I know what you mean. But how about . . . ?

The Six-Step Formula to overcome objections

Step 1 *Don't interrupt*
Never interrupt or pre-empt what the customer is trying to say, you might get it wrong. And always pause for a few seconds before replying because the customer might answer his own objection.

Step 2 *Throw it back*
Echo the customer's objection back to him. For example, if the customer says 'It's too much', throw it straight back to him in the form of a question: 'It's too much?' The customer will then explain himself or back down.

Step 3 *Show empathy or compliment*
Don't allow the customer to feel alienated. Instead show empathy, e.g. 'I understand how you feel but . . .' Alternatively compliment the customer to make him feel good, e.g. 'That's an excellent point, most people don't even think of that'.

Step 4 *Isolate*
Get the customer to agree that, other than the objection, he would be willing to go ahead and give it a try. Box the customer into a corner that he can't get out of.

Step 5 *Overcome*
Answer the objection.

Step 6 *Follow on/Close*
Continue on to the next subject in a nice smooth flowing manner, e.g. 'Did I tell you about . . . ?' Alternatively, if the customer has already been asked to buy, then close again, e.g. 'So let's give it a try?'

In the pages that follow there is a comprehensive list of the forty-two most common objections and the counters to overcome them. The first thing you must do when you hear an objection is determine whether it is genuine, or whether it is an excuse (a leak) or a flat no (a potato). I refer to an excuse as a leak because it gives the customer a hole to escape through, and I refer to a flat no as a potato because it is solid and weighs heavy on the stomach.

It is very important that you follow the Six-Step Formula whenever you get an objection. And remember, the only real reason that a customer doesn't buy should be lack of money.

Solutions to the forty-two most common objections

Index

How to Learn this Material

The key to learning is spaced repetition, going over something time and time again until it becomes second nature, just like when you learnt your multiplication tables at school

> One four is four,
> Two fours are eight,
> Three fours are twelve,
> Four fours are sixteen . . .

. . . over and over again, until it sticks, solid. Likewise, then, if you want to learn how to overcome customer objections, if you want to learn the counters and closes in this book, you must refer back to them time and time again, until they become second nature to you – until you become so conversant that you can reel off close after close without hesitation.

> To discover how to be a true pro-clo,
> Continue to learn and continue to grow.

Your income is derived from your professional skill – the more skill, the more income. You invested money to improve your skill when you bought this book, now you have to invest your time. Remember, the key to learning is spaced repetition. Don't try to cram everything in at once.

Instead, go over this material at regular intervals and you will add to your repertoire with each reading.

Quote
Benjamin Franklin once said: 'Empty the pennies from your purse into your mind and your mind will fill your purse with pennies.'
Practice makes perfect. DO IT!

Notes
Remember that the customer's name is music to his ears. Using the customer's name when closing creates warmth and sincerity, but be careful not to overdo it.

In Part Three, 'The Arsenal', there are many more closes which can be used to counter the forty-two objections listed here.

1   **It's too expensive – Objection. (Translation: I wonder if I can get the price down, or, I think I can get a better deal somewhere else.)**

Counter A   'You know, Mr Jones, our company came to a policy about price some years ago. We decided that it's better to explain our prices once, rather than apologize for quality for a lifetime. At the end of the day, you only ever get what you pay for, don't you agree? So, then, give it a try?'

Counter B   'Mr Jones, it's impossible to pay a little and get a lot, but tell me, would you rather have the cheapest solution or the best value for money? Then give it a try?'

Counter C   'It's too expensive?' (Echo the objection back to the customer as a question – force the customer to justify himself or back down.) This technique is covered in more detail on page 206 (The Echo Close).

2   **I want to think about it – Leak. (Translation: How am I going to get out of this? I need to slow things down. I didn't realize I was in so deep.)**

Counter A   'Mr Jones, if this (*product*) were free, you'd take it, wouldn't you? So the thing that's troubling you is the money, isn't that right?'

Counter B   'That's fine, Mr Jones, I'll leave you alone for a few minutes so that you can think things over while they're still fresh in your mind, and I'm still here to answer any of your questions. That's the most sensible thing to do, isn't it?

(You will find specific closes to overcome **I want to think about it** on pages 197 and 215)

3   **I want to compare it with others – Objection. (Translation: I'm sold and I'm going to buy but I want to check out the market-place first, to see what's on offer.)**

Counter A   Every product or service has features and benefits that are unique, that the competition doesn't have. When products are identical to that sold by the competition, the uniqueness will be found in the installation, or the after-sales service, or even the price.

To overcome this objection, you should use your unique selling points to convince the customer. For example:

> 'Mr Jones, you wouldn't accept a (*product*) that doesn't have this (*benefit*) would you?'
> 'And I'm sure you wouldn't accept a (*product*) of inferior quality to this one, would you?'
> 'Tell me, would you consider investing with a company that doesn't provide this (*service*)?'

Once you have got the customer to agree that he wouldn't accept anything less, to satisfy his needs, you should (if you haven't already) prove your product's uniqueness, and then close. (*Note:* A pro-clo knows his competition's product knowledge just as well as he knows his own.)

Counter B   'Mr Jones, it would take you a lifetime to compare it with every single (*product*) on the market. We have already agreed that the advantages and benefits of this (*product*) are what you are looking for, so don't pass it by, don't run the risk of losing out or paying more for it. Take advantage of this (*product*) now, and then by all means look around and compare it – for the next twelve months, if you like. That way, while you're looking around, you would be enjoying the benefits of this (*product*) at today's price. And of course, if you find something else that you prefer you can always sell (part-exchange, cash in, etc.). Mr Jones, you know that makes sense, so give it a try?'

Counter C   'Mr Jones, what will determine where you purchase?'

4   I want to speak to my solicitor first – Objection. (Translation: I'm sold but I want to check through the small print.)

Counter A   'OK, do you have his telephone number with you or shall I look it up in the book?'

Counter B   'You know, Mr Jones, many solicitors own this product but they don't read through the documentation because they know that if there were anything wrong with the agreement, if it was illegal or there were any misrepresentations, then the agreement would be null and void anyway. So give it a try?'

Counter C   'Tell me, if your solicitor was sitting here right now and he checked through everything and told you that everything was completely above board, would you be willing to go ahead? – Well, Mr Jones, I'm going to give you the opportunity to do just that. We'll do the paperwork now and secure the agreement with a deposit, then I will arrange to give you the time to take everything to your solicitor. If he finds

any misrepresentation whatsoever, we will
tear the agreement up and refund your
deposit in full. Fair enough?'

Counter D   'Mr Jones, your solicitor can't tell you
whether or not this is a good (*product*)
or advise you whether or not to go ahead
– he can only tell you if it's legal, and if
it weren't, we wouldn't be talking right
now, would we? So let's do it?'

5 I can't afford it - Objection or Leak or Condition. (Translation of objection or leak: I like it and I want one but not enough to part with my money.)

Counter A   'Exactly what is it that's causing a problem,
is it the deposit or the balance?' (Break it
down to money – find out what would be
comfortable.) 'Supposing, Mr Jones, that
your bank manager agreed to lend you the
money to invest in this (*product*), could you
manage a monthly amount of, say, £200 a
month?' (Reduce by small amounts until
the customer agrees that he could manage
that amount: £150? £125? £100? £90? etc.
Find out what the customer can afford
and if it's possible to offer finance for that
amount use the Sharp Angle Close on page
223.) 'If I could . . . would you?'

Counter B   'You can't afford it?' (The echo technique
again. This close is explained in detail on
page 206.)

Counter C   'Mr Jones, my question to you is, how can
                 you afford not to?'

(This objection is covered in more details on pages 196,
204–5, 220, 235 and 243.)

**6   You're pressurizing me – Leak. (Translation: Help, this
      is getting a little out of hand, I didn't realize this
      [*product*] was so good).**

Counter A   'Mr Jones, if you feel under pressure then
                 I apologize . . . but that pressure is com-
                 ing from yourself. You've seen what this
                 (*product*) will do for you. . . I know it
                 makes sense and so do you! All I want
                 is for you to join the many thousands
                 of satisfied customers we already have, so
                 how about it, Mr Jones, can we shake on
                 it?' (Offer your hand.)

Counter B   Respond with the De-Pressure Close on
                 page 238.

**7   I want to sleep on it – Leak. (Translation: Get me out
      of here before I end up buying. I'd much rather mull it
      over and see if I can find any drawbacks.)**

Counter A   'Mr Jones, the best time to make a decision
                 is when you have all the information in
                 front of you, don't you agree? Well, the
                 only time you have all the information at
                 your disposal is right now, whilst I'm here
                 and can answer any of your questions.

Now, what exactly is it that's bothering you?'

Counter B   'Mr Jones, if you leave here, you will try to justify in your mind every reason not to do it, rather than every reason to give it a try. You'll say to yourself "There's always next year", or "I'll come back next week". You know, Mr Jones, a wise decision can only be made now, when you have all the facts in front of you, so go ahead and give it a try?'

Counter C   'Mr Jones, there is no time like the present. If you can think of one good reason not to go ahead with this (*product*) right now, then don't do it – but tell me, what, if anything, would stop you?'

8   I'll be back – Leak. (Translation: I really like this salesperson and I don't want to hurt his feelings but I'm not 100 per cent sure about this.)

Counter A   'Mr Jones, you're not just saying that to get rid of me, are you? Then here, take my wallet/purse with you and bring it back when you return.' (This little ploy implies that you trust the customer with your money so it's only right that he should feel the same way about trusting you. The customer will not accept your wallet/purse – instead he will become awkward and hesitant. You should then continue with . . .) 'What is it that's really stopping you?'

Counter B   'Mr Jones, there's no time like the present, so why put it off, why not grab the bull by the horns and give it a try?'

9   I don't make on-the-spot decisions – Leak. (Translation: I don't want to do anything impulsive in case I make a mistake.)

Counter A   Mr Jones, that in itself is an on-the-spot decision that you've just made! Now, I'm not trying to be clever or funny but you've seen what this (*product*) will do for you, you've see how it works, you've seen how much money you will save and you've had all the information to enable you to make the right decision – so let's do it?'

Counter B   'Neither do I, Mr Jones, but we've spent a considerable amount of time going over this proposal with a fine tooth comb. I understand that you're a little hesitant but there is only one way you will ever find out what this is really like! Give it a try?'

10   I'm just not sure – Objection. (Translation: I'm almost there, but give me some more reassurance.)

Counter A   'Mr Jones, you will never be absolutely sure until you've tried it. If you go through life always uncertain and postponing things, you will never achieve anything, you'll end up being left on the shelf – so give it a try?'

Counter B   'Mr Jones, saving money makes sense,
                 doesn't it? Well, that's exactly what we
                 are talking about here, so let's do it?'

11 **I'm too old, if I were ten years younger . . . – Leak.
    (Translation: There's a good boy (pat, pat, pat), you've
    done an excellent job but I feel insecure.)**

Counter A   'Mr Jones, you're only as old as you feel
                 and besides, many of our customers are
                 a lot older than yourself. Right now, at
                 your stage of life, you should be treating
                 yourself and getting as much comfort and
                 enjoyment as you can. This (*product*) is
                 going to give you so much satisfaction and
                 happiness, so how about we start straight
                 away, what do you say?'

Counter B   'Mr Jones, God willing, you've got years
                 left yet, but one thing is for certain – you
                 can't take anything with you. This (*product*)
                 will not only provide you with a lot of
                 pleasure but it's a very good investment
                 for your family's future, so if nothing else
                 get it for them.'

Counter C   Respond with Close 41 – The Tape Meas-
                 ure Close – on page 229.

12 **I want to speak to my accountant/financial adviser –
    Objection or Leak. (Translation: I want to make sure
    it makes financial sense or thank you . . . but I'm out of
    here.)**

Counter A   'Mr Jones, your accountant can't decide whether you want this (*product*), he can only advise you how best to pay for it. The question is, would you like to have it?'

Counter B   'Mr Jones, there isn't an accountant in the world who is against saving money, so give it a try?'

Counter C   'I understand, Mr Jones, you want your accountant's advice on how to pay for it, isn't that right? OK, give me his number, I'll get him on the phone!'

Note: A pro-clo qualifies his leads properly, so that if a customer needs his accountant to make the decision (bona fide) the accountant would be in on the presentation.

13 I'm only looking – Leak. (Translation: Leave me alone, I'm scared stiff of buying – goodness me, is that the time!)

Counter A   'Mr Jones, you wouldn't be looking if you weren't interested, would you? Well, you can look until the cows come home but there is only one way you will ever find out what it's really like and that's by getting on board. So why don't you give it a try?'

Counter B   'I understand that, Mr Jones, but now you've looked and seen how much you would benefit from this (*product*), why don't you dip your feet in and get involved?'

14 **I've got too many commitments – I'm buying a new car, etc. – Leak, but almost a Potato. (Translation: I don't want one badly enough to sacrifice my hard-earned cash.)**

Counter A		'Mr Jones, we all have commitments and obligations and the timing will never be just right, but if you hesitate you will lose this (*option/product*) and possibly you'll never be able to get another. Mr Jones, don't put off tomorrow what you can do to-day – grab it while you can!'

Counter B		'Mr Jones, with all your other commitments, if this were comfortable for you financially, if we could fit this into your budget, without it taking food off your table, would you be willing to give it a try?'

15 **I can get it cheaper than that – Objection. (Translation: Sold, but is this the best price?)**

Counter A		'Mr Jones, tell me, which is more important to you, the cheapest solution or the best value for money?' (The answer will always be 'the best value for money'.) 'The cheapest solution wouldn't provide this, or that.' (You should reel off your product's unique selling points, as described in answering the objection **I want to compare** on page 159.) 'So you see, Mr Jones, although you can pick it up for less, you'd also be settling for less.

Now I know that you're not willing to accept second best, are you? Welcome aboard then!' (Offer handshake.)

Counter B 'Mr Jones, if, as you say, you can get this exact (*product*) from another company for less money, then I'd like a job with that company – who are they?'

Counter C 'All imitations are cheaper than the real thing, Mr Jones, aren't they? – I think I've made my point, so why don't we start the paperwork?'

16 We've just got married – we're too young – Leak. (Translation: Frightened of overcommitment.)

Counter A 'Mr and Mrs Jones, you're just starting out in life, what better time is there to plan for the future? Life is too short to spend it on the sidelines. You should start as you mean to go on – now give it a try?'

Counter B 'You now have a golden opportunity to better yourselves and invest in something worthwhile – an asset that will appreciate in value. Thousands of people would have given their right arm to have been able to get involved at your age. Don't miss out, get on the bandwagon now, while you still have the chance. How about it?'

17 I've just agreed to buy one off So-and-So, you're too

late – Objection, but sometimes a Condition. (Translation: If I had seen you first, you would have got the order.)

Counter A   'Mr Jones, if you could turn the clock back, tell me, which one would you have bought?' (The customer will always answer favourably because he feels obligation towards you. I am a firm believer in not knocking the competition, but if a customer has a preference for your goods, product, company, or service, then it is your obligation to cancel the deal with the competition and to fulfil the customer's preferences, with yourself.)

Counter B   'Mr Jones, instead of dealing with just one company, do you not think it would be wiser to use two? That way you are not tied to one individual, you can monitor the performances of both, whilst at the same time compare advantages and benefits? Besides, you would have two assets instead of one, so why not get this (*product*) as well and give us a try?'

18   **I want to speak to my parents, family, Tom, Dick, Harry – Objection or Leak. (Translation: I need some financial help, or, I'd like another opinion.)**

Counter A   'Supposing that you have talked to (*whoever*) and they thought it was a great idea, how would you handle the deposit?' (Bring it back to the money and the customer will more than likely forget about *whoever*.)

Counter B   'Tell me, Mr Jones, would I be right in
             thinking that you want to speak to (*who-
             ever*) about the money side of things? So
             what exactly is the problem?'

19 I'm looking for/on behalf of somebody else – Leak. (Translation: I must try to throw him off the scent.)

Counter A   'That's great, Mr Jones, our best form
             of advertising is by word of mouth and
             we do a tremendous amount of business
             from referrals, but tell me, now you've seen
             what we have to offer, don't you feel it is
             something that you would like to have?'

Counter B   'Tell me, Mr Jones, what, if anything, would
             stop you personally from going ahead with
             this (*product*)?'

Counter C   'I'll check in a minute and see if I can find
             them for you, but how about it, Mr Jones,
             are you happy to go ahead?'

20 It's too big, too small, I don't like this, that, etc. – Objection. (Translation: I want it but . . .)

Counter A   'Tell me, Mr Jones, on what will you base
             your decision? On the fact that it's a little
             bigger than you prefer, or the overall ad-
             vantages and benefits of the (*product*)?'

Counter B   'If I could find you a smaller one (larger

one, different colour, etc.), would you be
willing to give it a try?'

**21 I just don't feel right – I don't really want it – Potato.
(Translation: Tough luck, sonny, better luck next time.)**

Counter A   'Exactly what is it you're not sure about,
               what is it that's stopping you?'

Counter B   'Mr Jones, if we were giving this (*prod-
               uct*) away for free, you'd want one then,
               wouldn't you? So what we're really talking
               about is the money, isn't it?'

Counter C   'Mr Jones, this (*product*) is only for people
               who are interested in investing in quality
               while at the same time saving money. Is
               having quality and saving money important
               to you? Well then, give it a try?'

**22 I want a discount – Objection. (Translation: Give me
your best deal, treat me special, and I'll buy.)**

Counter A   'I'm sorry, Mr Jones, our prices are fixed
               but I'll tell you what I'll do – (throw in
               a freebie) I'll treat you to a meal, on me!
               Now, how about it?'

Counter B   'If you take two, I can give you a 10 per
               cent discount which is, in effect, the saving
               on our marketing costs. When do you want
               to take delivery?'

23 I'm not buying today – we can't decide today – Objection. (Translation: Hang on a minute – I'm sold but I'm frightened of taking the plunge!)

Counter A 'Mr Jones, I don't want you to buy it or decide today, I want you to get involved and try it first. I don't want you to decide and pay cash, but rather get on board with our easy payment scheme, try it for a while and, in effect, defer your decision until you've tasted what it's like. It might be that it's not for you, in which case you can liquidate your asset without having paid for it in full. (You can sell it, part-exchange it, upgrade or downgrade it, etc.) Mr Jones, nothing ventured is nothing gained, so give it a try?'

Counter B 'Mr Jones, deciding not to decide is a decision, so you can do it. But in essence, as we've already agreed over a period of time you will spend this amount of money – that decision has already been made. Mr Jones, it's not a decision but a choice – what would you rather do, save (invest) money and enjoy the benefits of owning this (*product*), or would you rather continue as you are, throwing money down the drain? You know it makes sense, so make the right choice and shake my hand?' (Offer the customer your hand.)

24 **We don't have the budget for it – Leak. (Translation: Sorry folks, not today, come back next year. Leave me alone, there's a good chap, otherwise I might end up buying.)**

Counter A   'Mr Jones, if it were in the budget, would you have gone ahead?' (The customer, thinking he is off the hook, will readily agree.) 'Then how about if we place an order now, for four months' time, when you get your new budget? All I need is an order number (or a small securing deposit) and that way we can guarantee not only a delivery date but the price as well. – What order number shall I use?'

Counter B   'Mr Jones, I don't think there's a company in the world who wouldn't allow or permit over-expenditure of the budget to buy a product (or service) that will give it an edge over the competition, a product that will make the company more efficient and ultimately more profitable. Mr Jones, don't you agree that it would be worthwhile overlooking the budget in this case?'

25 **We've been doing business with So-and-So for years – we're satisfied – Objection. (Translation: Better the devil you know than the one you don't – I'd like to . . . but I can't justify a change.)**

Counter A   'Mr Jones, after all those years you've been doing business with So-and-So, it would be unreasonable for me expect you to stop dealing with them and instead deal with ourselves. But how about giving us a piece of your business, try us out as a second supplier, and allow us the chance to show you what we can do? That way, instead of having all your eggs in one basket, you will create a bit of healthy competition and benefit from it. Mr Jones, what have you got to lose – give us a try?'

Counter B   'Mr Jones, I appreciate that you have been dealing with So-and-So for years and that you are satisfied with their service, but am I right in thinking that years ago, when you chose to do business with So-and-So, you did so because you were concerned with value, quality and service?' (The customer can only agree, and possibly add more fuel to the fire by voicing more concerns that he was interested in.) 'Why, then, Mr Jones, would you deny yourself the opportunity of trying us out and deny yourself the benefit of comparing the value, quality and service of the goods we supply? Why not allow us to prove to you that we are second to none – give us a try?'

Counter C   'Mr Jones, tell me, what do I have to do to get your business?'

26 **Can I take some literature to mull over? – Leak, bordering on becoming a Potato. (Translation: Leave me alone and stop pestering me.)**

Counter A   (Assume the sale.) 'Of course you can, I'll

give you lots of brochures so that you can show off your new (*product*) to your family and friends.' (Without hesitating, continue with Close 34, The Order Form Close, on page 221.)

Counter B   'Mr Jones, our literature won't give you the answers you're looking for . . . so tell me, what is it that's bothering you?'

27 I have a friend/relative in the trade, I'd like to consult them – Leak. (Translation: I'm not sure about this, I'd like another professional opinion.)

Counter A   'I understand, Mr Jones, that you want to be sure that you're making the right choice. But what is it that's actually troubling you? Is it this benefit, is it that benefit (is it all the things we have agreed upon), is it the money?' (Bring it back to the money again.)

Counter B   'If your friend were here with us right now and he were to ask you how you felt, I'm pretty certain you'd tell him you felt it was a good deal, wouldn't you? Well, Mr Jones, if your friend is a real friend, he would only want what is best for you, so why don't you give it a try?'

28 I want to pray – I want to speak to God – Objection. (Translation: It seems OK . . . but to be on the safe side, I'd like to ask for direction from above.)

Counter A   'I understand, Mr Jones. Would you like me to take you somewhere quiet or leave you alone for a few minutes?'

Counter B   'I understand, Mr Jones, you want to make sure that you don't make a bad decision. Well, let's look at the worst possible scenario.' (Continue with Close 38, Worst Scenario Close, on page 226.)

29 I'm not in any hurry – Potato. (Translation: Don't call us, we'll call you.)

Counter A   'Neither am I, Mr Jones, so let's take our time with the paperwork. Now just to be sure, how do you spell your surname?'

Counter B   'Mr Jones, from what you have seen and from what we've discussed, do you agree that this would save you money? So when do you feel is the best time to cut costs and start saving money, now or in the future?'

30 I don't have the deposit with me, I'll come back later – Leak. (Translation: Phew! This is a little too close for comfort, I need a 'breather', I need a way out.)

Counter A   'Don't worry about the deposit now, Mr Jones. We'll do the paperwork first and we'll sort out the deposit later.' (Once the paperwork is signed, sealed and delivered, you should arrange the deposit or go with the customer to collect it.)

31 A colleague of mine had a bad experience with your product/company – Objection. (Translation: Reassure me and I'm all yours.)

Counter A   There are three steps to overcoming this objection.

Step 1   Find out what the problem was with the product, company, or salesperson.

Step 2   Have the customer answer his own objection – you should say: 'Mr Jones, if you were the managing director of our company and this problem occurred, what would you have done about it?'

Step 3   Whatever the customer says, agree with it – say: 'That's exactly what we did, now why don't you give it a try?'

Counter B   'Mr Jones, we've all had our fair share of problems at one time or another and we've all made more than a few mistakes in our time, after all, we wouldn't be human if we hadn't. But to succeed you have to learn from those mistakes so they don't happen again, don't you agree?' (Proceed to then show the customer how you've made amends and ask for the order.)

32 I'll get back to you – leave it with me – I'll let you know – Leak, bordering on becoming a Potato. (Translation: Which is the way out, get me out of here!)

Counter A   'Mr Jones, what, if anything, would stop

you from taking advantage of this (*product*) right here and now?'

Counter B   'Fine, Mr Jones, let me just get my diary and we'll make another appointment.' (When the customer flounders, say:) 'So tell me, what is it that's stopping you, what is it that you're not happy with?'

33 **I don't want to buy anything – Potato. (Translation: I don't want one. However, if a customer said this to you at the beginning of the sales presentation, he is trying to throw you off track, he knows he is game for a good deal and he is frightened of being sold.)**

Counter A   'Mr Jones, when you buy something that money is spent, gone for ever. With this, you're not spending money that's gone for ever, you're investing in an asset that will pay you dividends for as long as you keep it. Mr Jones, I don't want you to buy it, I want you to invest in it. Now give it a try?'

Counter B   'Mr Jones, everybody is for cutting costs and saving money. Right now you are looking a gift horse in the mouth and you know it – so give it a try?'

34 **It's not the right time – we're in the process of moving house, etc. – Leak. (Translation: Maybe some other time – I'm not sold enough to buy.)**

Counter A   'Mr Jones, it's never the right time. If you wait for just the right time to come, it never will. I appreciate that you have commitments and finances might be a little tight right now, but you can't afford to let this go by. You must grab this opportunity while you can – so give it a try?'

Counter B   'Let me ask you, when is the right time?' (Await response.) 'So, if we placed the order today and secured it with a small holding deposit, but we allowed you to pay the balance (*whenever*), you would be willing to give it a try, wouldn't you?'

Counter C   'How about if I could arrange to have this (*product*) financed with your new mortgage, so you would hardly feel it! You'd have it then, wouldn't you?'

35 I need it by Tuesday – I want what you can't give me. – Objection. (Translation: If you can't give it to me, I'll find somebody else who can.)

Counter A   (Assuming you can't supply but the competition can.) 'Mr Jones, from our discussion it's obvious that this (*product*) is the one that best suits your needs. Instead of improvising and accepting second best now, doesn't it make more sense to wait until you can get what you really need?'

Counter B   Respond with Close 2, the Concession Close, page 194.

36 I'm concerned about . . . How do I know it will do what you say it will do? – Objection. (Translation: It's a big step, help me to trust you – sell me some more.)

Counter A   'Mr Jones, I understand your concern about (*whatever*), but if I could assure you, 100 per cent, that this won't happen, would you be willing to go ahead?'

Counter B   'Mr Jones, if I could prove to you beyond any shadow of a doubt that this (*product*) will do everything we say it will – do we have a deal?'

After both these responses you should overcome the customer's concern. Then, assuming the sale, start the paperwork.

37 Let me sleep on it and I might buy ten tomorrow – Leak, bordering on becoming a Potato. (Translation: I've got to shake this guy off – I feel boxed in.)

Counter A   'Mr Jones, I don't doubt your sincerity and I know you wouldn't say that if you weren't serious about owning this (*product*). However, rather than being impulsive, don't you feel it would be better to start small, try it out first, then you can always add more later. That makes more sense, doesn't it?'

Counter B   'Mr Jones, are you being genuine or are you trying to fob me off? Then to show me how sincere you are, why don't you start with one, right now?'

38 I don't like it – Potato. (Translation: Tough cookies – better luck next time.)

Counter A   'What makes you say that?' or 'You don't like it?' (Echo.)

Counter B   'Mr Jones, if I could give you ten of these (*product*) free, how many would you have? So it's not that you don't like it – it's the money that you're concerned about, isn't it?' (Bring it back to the money.)

39 I'm sorry, but it's not for me – Potato (Translation: Polite way of saying 'Get lost'.)

Counter A   'Mr Jones, I can give you umpteen different reasons why this is for you and why you should have it – because of this (benefit) and because of that (benefit), because earlier you said you wanted to be able to improve performance, because this will give you quality and . . .' (Continue to list all the owner benefits swiftly.) 'But, Mr Jones, I can't think of one good reason why it's not for you . . . can you? Then give it a try?'

Counter B   'Tell me, Mr Jones, why do you feel it's not for you?'

40 It's too much to take in all at once – you don't expect me to buy now, today? – Leak. (Translation: I thought you were my friend – don't change into a salesman.)

Counter A   'Mr Jones, aside from the money, what would stop you from going ahead today?'

Counter B   'Mr Jones, this (*product*) isn't complicated and at the end of the day (presentation, demonstration) everyone knows whether or not it's something they would like to have. I think this is a case of the old pounds, shillings and pence, isn't it?'

41 I'm not signing anything today – Objection. (Translation: I'm frightened.)

Counter A   'That's fine, Mr Jones, we can do the paperwork tomorrow ... but as we're going ahead we'll need a securing deposit of £100 today. How do you want to handle it?'

Counter B   'Tell me, Mr Jones, what is it you're afraid of?'

Counter C   Respond with Close 34, The Work Sheet (Order Form) Close, on page 221.

42 I don't like finance – Objection. (Translation: I don't like paying interest, or, I don't want a debt hanging around my neck.)

Counter A   'Mr Jones, don't think of it as finance, think of it as a pension scheme, a savings account, or a catalogue club. You put so much a week, or a month, into your account and you benefit from owning the (*product*), but at any time you like you

can always close the account (pay it off
or sell it). Everybody does it this way –
so, give it a try?'

Counter B   'Mr Jones, by not owning this (*product*)
it's costing you money (health, comfort,
lost production, etc.) and that cost is 100
per cent interest. On the other hand, when
you own the (*product*) it still costs you
interest, but nowhere near 100 per cent.
Tell me, what would you rather do, pay
100 per cent interest or just a fraction
of that? – Then give it a try?'

RECAP

1   An *objection* is a statement of interest, a veiled request
for more information.

2   A *condition* is a genuine reason that stops the customer
from going ahead (normally lack of money).

3   A *leak* is an excuse not to go ahead. Here the customer
feels some obligation, but not enough. In this situation
there is generally a lot more work to do.

4   A *potato* is a flat no. Here it is obviously very difficult,
if not impossible, to close the sale.

Whenever you receive an objection, determine which of
the above it is and then follow the Six-Step Formula.

Step 1 Don't interrupt or pre-empt what the customer is
trying to say.

Step 2 Throw it back in the form of a question.

Step 3 Show empathy or compliment.

Step 4 Isolate the objection – box the customer into a corner.

Step 5 Overcome, answer the objection.

Step 6 Follow on to another subject or close the sale.

PART THREE

The Arsenal (Closes)

Closing

Anybody can sell, but it's closing that makes the sale.

This next section is going to show you how to do just that, close the sale. You are about to discover some of the secret weapons of the pro-clo, you will find revelations that will make you rich beyond your wildest dreams and you will be given the means to ensure a lifetime of success and prosperity. You are about to voyage into a world of vintage secrets, where you will find an arsenal of closes bottled up and ready for your use. You are now well on your way to becoming part of an exclusive breed, you're about to become a fully fledged pro-clo and I'll be with you every step of the way – to welcome you into the elite top 5 per cent, the domain of the PRO-CLO!

Before plunging into this exciting section, take note of these very important points.

1   Again in this section, there are numerous examples, and for ease and simplicity, I have restricted myself to the use of he or him rather than using, literally hundreds of times, he/she or him/her. This use of the masculine pronoun is by no means meant to be derogative or chauvinistic. I think it only fair to point out that some of the best closers I have ever met are women, my wife and daughter included.

189

2   As mentioned earlier in this book (Step 36), whenever
     a pro-clo asks a closing question he must shut up,
     he must be silent and remain that way, resisting the
     pressure to speak again until after the customer has
     responded. I cannot stress the importance of this point
     enough.

3   Closing is an intimate time, so use the customer's
     name for warmth and sincerity – not so much the
     Mr and Mrs that I have used in my examples but
     more the customer's forename.

4   It is my experience that only 5 per cent of salespeople
     continue to persevere after the fourth rejection. On
     average, these top 5 per cent of all salespeople, these
     top professional closers, will receive five no's be-
     fore they receive a yes. To get five no's before a
     yes, they have to use six closes.

5   The pro-clo is forever learning new techniques and
     new closes. He knows that to succeed and continuously
     prosper, he must know more ways of getting to yes
     than the customer knows ways of saying no. Here,
     instead of describing six closes, there are sixty different
     proven closes for everyday use. Learn them, and add
     variety and excitement and charisma to your closing
     library. Learn them until you become so conversant
     that you are able to flow from one to another without
     hesitation. If you only learn one of these closes and
     you use it, this book will pay for itself many thou-
     sands of time over, but if you learn them all and use
     them, you're going to be rich!

6   This section is an accumulation of closes. Some are old

favourites, others I have picked up and adapted and some are of my own creation. With such a wide collection to choose from, you will always find something suitable for every customer and every occasion.

7   Being a good salesperson is never good enough, you have to be a good closer as well. It's no good just selling a customer on a product, you have to close him into buying it. Likewise it's no good just learning these closes, you have to use them constantly, otherwise you will forget them.

8   I've often heard it said that the top salesperson, the professional closer, is a lucky s.o.b. I believe this statement to be absolutely true because luck comes to those who prepare.

PREPARE YOURSELF!

Sixty proven closes for everyday use

Index   *page*

1 The Alternative Choice Close

This close is one of the most popular all-time favourites, simply because it works extremely well when executed properly. In this close we assume that the customer is going to buy and we don't give him the option to answer yes or no to our questions.

We simply give the customer a choice of two options. (*Note:* If you give customers more than two options you run the risk of confusing them, and the more you confuse them the more likely you are to get the objection 'We want to think about it'.) The perception of the pro-clo tells him in advance which of the two options the customer is likely to choose, but in a lot of cases there isn't really a choice

at all, as one of the options will be heavily loaded against.
This is how the Alternative Choice Close works.

'So, from the options we have discussed, would you
rather take advantage of the policy giving you maximum life cover (pause) or would you prefer the
policy giving you adequate life cover with maximum
investment and a tax free lump sum at maturity?'

'Are you more favourable towards the green or the
blue?'

'Would you rather start with two weeks taking advantage of the special price or just the one week?'

'Would you be happier arranging your own finance
or taking our easy payment scheme?'

Once the customer has chosen his option, you then proceed by asking *the closing question,* however you want
to phrase it, e.g. 'Providing I can get approval on that,
are you happy to go ahead?'

'If I could . . . are you willing to give it a try? OK –
welcome aboard!' (Offer your hand.)

2 The Concession Close

Only use this close when the customer is at the stage
where he is almost sold on the product, he is teetering
on the edge and needs that extra little something to tip
him over.
   (*Note:* You must never appear weak by giving too
much away, as the customer might feel that you're getting

desperate, there's a catch, or it sounds too good to be true, and then he will not buy.)

The Concession Close sometimes works best when you intimate that you're not sure whether you will be able to give the concession (although you know full well that you are). The customer then feels he has achieved something, which makes him more agreeable and keeps the sale sold.

Here are some examples of how the Concession Close works.

'If I can jump the queue and have a delivery here by Monday, can I have your order today?'

'If I could get you that model in metallic grey for the same price, do we have a deal?'

'As our available inventory is extremely limited, I really don't know whether or not this would be possible, but . . . if I could find you an ex-display model at the old price, would you take it?'

Tit-for-tat concession

This takes things one step further and works on the principle that nothing is for free – if you offer something you receive something in return. This makes any justification for a concession easier to make. As an example:

'If I could get you the new model at the old price, would you be willing to take four instead of two?'

'If I could spread the cost over three months, would you take the deluxe version instead of the standard?'

3 The Testing the Water Close

This close is useful when the customer is struggling with
the money. He just can't afford to buy the one he prefers,
but his pride won't let him admit that to you. Besides,
he doesn't want to accept second best. This close is also
very effective with the customer who is apprehensive or
frightened of taking the plunge.

The scenario you put to the customer shows him that
you have his best interests in mind, it makes his decision
that much easier and allows the customer to justify to
himself a lesser option. This close actually takes the customer's mind off whatever is troubling him for a minute
or two and allows you to recondition the customer's
feelings and thought-patterns.

Here's how it works.

'Mr Jones, I'd like to put this scenario to you. Imagine taking an inflatable boat over a reef. Now you
wouldn't just open her up full throttle and plough
across the water as fast as you can, because the water
might be too shallow or there could be something
obstructing your path. What you should do is test
the water first, you should make sure that it's safe,
and then when you're comfortable and confident
that you can handle it, you can always come back
as fast as you like. The same principle applies now
with this (*product*). Rather than full steam ahead,
it would be better to test the water first, feel your
way and try it to begin with.'

Once you've taken the initiative in suggesting that the customer begins slowly, you should then proceed by making
a proposal, tying it down with the closing question:

'I think it would be better to start with four boxes instead of six, don't you?'

'I feel we would be wiser starting with the one week first, then we can always look to adding on an additional week at a later date, don't you agree?'

'If we started by replacing the windows in the front of the house, which is the most important, we could always do the rear of the house a few months down the road. That would be the best option, wouldn't it?'

4 The Winston Churchill Close (also known as Ben Franklin)

This one is for the thinker who deliberately ponders, or the customer who just wants to think about it.

The close is demonstrated on paper but also works well in a simplified verbal fashion. We'll look at both versions.

Here's how this close is used.

'Mr Jones, in the UK Winston Churchill has always been regarded as one of our wisest men. Whenever he had a problem, or a decision to make, and he wasn't sure what to do, he would take a piece of paper and draw a line down the middle of it. On one side of the paper he would write the word "yes", and on the other side the word "no". Then, Churchill would list all the good and beneficial factors and favourable points for the decision under the "yes" column, and all the reasons against in the "no" column.

'When he had finished this exercise, he would simply

add up the yes's and no's. If there were more yes's he'd give it the green light and go ahead. If there were more no's he'd give it the red light and decline. Mr Jones, it certainly can't hurt, let's try it?'

(*Note:* You should tactfully assist the customer on the 'yes' side by making suggestions such as the owner benefits or bonus features, etc., but on the 'no' side you should stay quiet and not offer any assistance. The 'yes' side will always win!)

Once this process is complete, you must then ask for the order:

'Well, Mr Churchill, do we get the green light?'

'There it is in black and white . . . give it a try?' (Nod your head slightly, outstretch your hand and be silent.)

'Well, that about sums it up, welcome aboard.' (Hand out.)

Sometimes, especially on a cold sales call, the Winston Churchill Close demonstrated on paper can be a little long-winded, in which case the customer may become bored or irritable. To speed things up and keep the flow going, use the Winston Churchill Close verbal fashion:

'You know, Mr Jones, in the UK Winston Churchill has always been regarded as one of our wisest and most intelligent leaders. Whenever he had a problem or a decision to make and he wasn't sure what to do, he would simply weigh up the fors and againsts and whichever came out on top would decide whether he would give it the green light or the red. Now, we've discussed ten, maybe twenty reasons why this (*product*) is for you. (You should then proceed to reel off, without hesitating, as many owner benefits or positive reasons as you can.) . . . But I can't think of one reason that would stop you from going ahead.'

Now, pause for a second or two, and see if the customer comes up with a reason for not going ahead. If the customer states an objection, overcome it and then try another close. If after you have paused for a second or two the customer remains silent, then you proceed as before: 'Well, Mr Churchill, do we get the green light?'

5 The Fear Close

This is a pressure close used to create urgency. This close is most effective with the customer who is sold on the product, but maybe not yours, or the customer who knows he is going to buy one, but goodness gracious, you mean now? What, today?

At the beginning of the sales presentation the customer's fear of losing will be greater than his expectation of gaining (think about that), which is why the customer puts up his defence shield to protect himself. At the end of the sales presentation, providing the pro-clo has done his job, the opposite occurs. The customer's expectation of gaining will be greater than his fear of losing, which is why he buys.

However, sometimes there is an in-between, when the customer is fifty-fifty, neither for nor against – or, to put it another way, the value of the product and its benefits are not quite worth enough for the customer to part with his money.

The Fear Close will create the extra desire needed to clinch the sale. (*Note:* You must be genuine and at your

most convincing, otherwise you will sound false and will
lose credibility and the sale.)

Here are a few examples.

> 'Mr and Mrs Smith, who referred us to you, were
> so excited and happy about the prospect of you also
> owning the product. Let's not disappoint them? (One-
> second pause.) Give it a try?' (Hand out – shut up.)

In the above example, the fear is of ridicule, of losing face
with Mr and Mrs Smith – peer pressure.

> 'God forbid, but if anything should happen before
> you've decided, imagine what the consequences would
> be. Let's not tempt fate. If you go ahead now, you
> will be covered immediately. How about it?'

In this example the fear is of dreadful consequences,
due to lack of cover – security.

> 'As I explained earlier, Mr Jones, we only have two
> of these units left at this price. Well, the couple over
> there on your right have just bought one which
> means there is now only one left. If you hesitate you
> could lose it and the discount worth £300. (Pause
> one second.) Give it a try?'

In the above example, the fear is of loss, of losing out on
that special deal, of being pipped at the post – greed.

6 The Safety in Numbers Close

Most people like to think of themselves as pioneers of a
sort, but in reality, very few are willing to take that first

step into the unknown. The path of proven success is one that is always a lot easier to follow.

This close is used on the customer who is timid, or unsure, or cautious and insecure, or the customer who is doubtful. It uses third-party stories to demonstrate familiarization and safety in numbers. For example:

'Tell me something, Mr Jones, do you know John Smith from ABC Limited? Well, he got involved with us about three months ago, and he is so happy with our product that yesterday he ordered another one. Now, they say that the "proof is in the pudding", so let me ask you, do you think that ABC Limited would have ordered another (*product*) if they weren't totally satisfied with what we have to offer?' (The customer will answer with 'I guess not'.) 'So, then, give it a try?'

'You know, Mr Jones, I have a client called Mr Smith, who like yourself has recently suffered from ill-health. Well, Mr Smith had his conservatory installed almost three years ago and he is now fully recovered. In this recent letter (produce letter) to me, Mr Smith says that he feels that the pleasure and happiness he has enjoyed in his conservatory has greatly contributed to his recovery. Mr Jones, if it worked for Mr Smith, it could work for you. (One-second pause.) Now, can I have your approval to go ahead?'

'Mr Jones, over three thousand homes in this local area have had this security system installed, because with the escalating crime rates a deterrent is almost a necessity. For your own piece of mind, let's do it?'

Comparison Closing

Analogy or comparison closing is fun and highly successful providing you keep it simple, light and entertaining. These closes are used to get the customer to 'see the light' and become converted. Here is a sample of some of my favourites.

7 The Bicycle Close

'Mr Jones, this (*product*) is an investment and like any investment, the longer you keep it, the more it's worth. It's like getting on a bicycle. The longer you pedal it for, the farther you are going to go, but at any time you like you can always stop and get off. Likewise, with this (*product*). The longer you keep it, the farther you are going to go (or the more it will be worth), but at any time you like you can always cash it in (or sell it) and get off. First of all, though, you have to climb on and start pedalling. So, why not give it a try?'

8 The Savings Account Close

'Mr Jones, don't think of this as money being spent, because it's not, it's only invested. At any time you feel like it, you can always cash it in or sell it. It's just like a savings account. You put so much money aside each month into this savings account. While the account's open, you get the benefits of the product. And if you decide to close the account at a later date, you get a lump sum return. So, I am not asking you to spend money and buy it, I am asking you to invest and to give it a try.'

9 The First Class Close

'Mr Jones, there's first class and there's economy class. At the end of the day, they both work out to be the same price, so the choice is yours – but as there's no difference in the long run, we should take the first class route, don't you agree?'

10 The Pension Close

'Mr Jones, this is just like a private pension scheme, inasmuch as you put monthly contributions into it. The only difference is, you don't have to wait until you retire to receive the benefits – you get the benefits from day one, plus you have an asset that is growing all the time. Mr Jones, you know this makes sense, so let's do it?'

11 The Big Toe Close

'Mr Jones, when you take a bath, you don't just jump in, you dip your big toe in first and wiggle it around to make sure the water's OK. That's what I'm asking you to do now, dip your toe in and try it. Then if you like it, you can always get in a little deeper. That makes more sense, doesn't it?'

12 The Logic Close

'Mr Jones, for £300 or £400 a month you can own a nice house, or for the same amount of money you can rent one from the council. Either way, you can have a beautiful home, but we all know which makes more sense. (*Note:* Not to be used on tenants.) Similarly with a car, you pay for it over a period, or use the same money to rent one. Either way, you get a nice car, but again, we know which makes more sense. (One-second pause.) Likewise, Mr Jones, with this (*product*) you can see all the advantages and benefits and you know it makes sense. So give it a try?'

13 The New Company Close

'Mr Jones, what I'd like you to do is to look at this as if you were considering buying shares in a new company. Instead of buying in lock, stock and barrel, you would do better to try them out first, monitor the company's performance and see how they do. That way, if you're not happy with them you get rid of them, but if they perform exceptionally well you can get further involved. Mr Jones, if you try us out as a new supplier you certainly haven't got anything to lose, but you've got everything to gain. How about if I put you down for five to start with, or shall we keep it even numbers and start with half a dozen?'

Note
The next three closes are for use when you have to sell down (less), usually due to lack of money.

14 The Walk Before We Run Close

'You know, Mr Jones, we all learn to walk before we run. It's nature's way of protecting us from moving too fast too soon. We have to find our feet first, and then as we become more confident we advance. Likewise with this (*product*), almost everyone starts with one or two and then adds on later. It's a natural progression. (Make the customer feel that this situation is normal and completely acceptable.) I think it would be better if we started with this one, wouldn't it?'

15 The Ladder Close

'You know, Mr Jones, it's a lot easier to start on the bottom rung of the ladder and climb upwards than it is to start at the top and climb down. Instead of jumping in at the deep end, it might be better if you started slowly by taking this option first. Then you could try it out, and if you wanted to, get involved further at a later date. I think this one would be far better suited to you, wouldn't it?'

16 The Jumper Close

'Imagine, Mr Jones, that you want to buy a jumper. The first thing you do is find something that you like the look of. Then you pick it up and feel its texture. Then you check the label for the size and to see how it will wash. Finally, you try it on before you take it. Now, once you've worn that jumper a couple of times, if you're happy with the quality, the chances are, you will go back to the shop and buy another one. My company works on the same principle. We feel you should try it first, then, if you're happy with it, you'll come back for more. Besides, it also means that your initial investment is greatly reduced, which

makes it a lot easier, doesn't it? So, do you still want
it delivered, or are you going to collect it?'

17 The Echo Close (also known as the Porcupine)

This is an absolute gem, and one of the simplest of
closes to use. The Echo or Porcupine Close is used to get
an insight into the customer's thoughts and feelings. This
close never fails to get a response. It works by answering a
question with a question. If you stand in front of a mirror
and smile, your reflection smiles straight back at you, and
it's on the same principle that the Echo Close works. When
a customer asks a question or states an objection, you
echo it, you throw it straight back, but in a puzzled tone
of voice and with a somewhat surprised expression. The
customer then has to justify the objection, and in doing
so he will either answer himself or give the pro-clo the
information he needs to close the sale.

This is best illustrated by way of examples.

CUSTOMER: 'I can't afford it.'
PRO-CLO: 'You can't afford it?' (Remain silent and
             the customer will justify or explain him-
             self. Many salespeople jump in or say
             something like: 'Well, I know it's expen-
             sive but . . . blah! blah! blah!')
CUSTOMER: 'What I mean is, I can't afford to do it now.
             I'd have to wait until next month.'

CUSTOMER: 'It's more than I thought.'
PRO-CLO: 'It's more than you thought?'

CUSTOMER: 'It doesn't feel right.'
PRO-CLO: 'It doesn't feel right?'

Once the question or objection has been answered, you must ask the customer to give it a try. Let's run through a sequence.

CUSTOMER: 'It's too much.' (Objection)
PRO-CLO: 'It's too much?' (Echo)
CUSTOMER: 'It's just out of my league, I just can't afford it.' (Justification)
PRO-CLO: 'By how much is it too much?'
CUSTOMER: 'By a long way, I just couldn't manage it.'
PRO-CLO: 'I understand, Mr Jones, but what seems to be the stumbling block, is it the £300 initial deposit or the £150 a month?' (Alternative Choice)
CUSTOMER: 'Well, I could scrape together the deposit, but no way could I manage £150 a month, not with my mortgage and car.'
PRO-CLO: 'How much could you manage a month?'
CUSTOMER: 'I could manage maybe half that amount. Say, £70 a month.'
PRO-CLO: 'We would have to look towards remortgaging, but if I could get it down to £70 a month, are you willing to give it a try?' (Sharp Angle Close)

18 The ABC Close

This is the easiest close of all, as easy as ABC. I call it that because it is a three-question close. This close is used after a nice smooth presentation, when you haven't received too much in the way of negative responses or objections.

This is how the ABC Close works.

Step A

> PRO-CLO: 'Do you have any questions?'
> CUSTOMER: 'No, I don't think so.'

Step B

> PRO-CLO: 'So you're happy with every-
>   thing, then?'
> CUSTOMER: 'Well, yes, I suppose so.'

Step C

> PRO-CLO: 'Good, welcome aboard.' (Out-
>   stretch hand.)

or

Step A

> PRO-CLO: 'Is there anything you would like
>   me to go over again?'
> CUSTOMER: 'No, I've got it.'

Step B

> PRO-CLO: 'Are you happy with everything,
>   then?' (Nodding.)
> CUSTOMER: 'Yes.'

Step C

> PRO-CLO: 'OK, let's give it a try?' (Out-
>   stretch hand.)
>   'Can we go ahead, then?'
>   'Great, so you're willing to go
>   for it, then?'
>   'Do we have a deal?'
>   'Would you prefer to take it now
>   or have us deliver?'
>   'So, there is nothing stopping
>   us going ahead now, is there?'

Subtle pressure closing

The following closes should only be used in certain circumstances and with great care. Remember, a pro-clo doesn't push his customers, he pulls them. So when using these closes to create subtle pressure, do it in a humorous way, with a smile on your face.

Subtle pressure closes can be used in the following instances:

1   When a customer is being laid back and nonchalant.
2   When a customer is trying to be clever in front of his/her partner.
3   When there is no customer reaction.
4   When a customer is being very indecisive.
5   When one party is sold and the other isn't (usually she is, he isn't).

Here are some examples of subtle pressure closes.

19 The Dimwit Close

'Mr Jones, you would have to be either a dimwit or completely crazy not to see the potential of this (*product*), don't you agree? – So, then, give it a try?'

20 The Money Talks Close

Be genuine and sincere with this one, otherwise your customer will get up and walk off. Make sure your tone is friendly, and smile.

'Mr Jones, money talks and wafflers walk . . . shall

I see if I can find something a little better priced?'
(Raise your eyebrows and nod.)

21 The 'Even a Child Could Do It' Close

'Mr Jones, this (*product*) works out at £2 a day.
When was the last time you were offered ownership of (*product*) for £2 a day (less than the price
of a packet of cigarettes)? You know, Mr Jones,
I'll bet a child could make more than that washing
cars after school. If a child can do it, I am sure
that you can, so give it a try?'

22 The Honeymoon Close (she's sold, he isn't sure)

'You know, Mr and Mrs Jones, if you don't mind
my saying, you two are just so well matched, you
seem so compatible and happy together. (Be serious
and sincere. No joking, and don't let the customer
interrupt.) Do you remember, Mr Jones, when you
got married, how much in love you were, how excited
and happy you were? (Don't hesitate, keep going.)
Imagine on your honeymoon, your wife had asked
you to get this (*product*) for her. If you could have
afforded it then, and knowing how much you loved
her, you would have bought it for her, wouldn't
you? (Now smile and say:) So tell me, Mr Jones,
do you love your wife any less today? (Watch the
wife look at him.) Then for her sake, let's give it a
whirl?'

23 The Liars or Buyers Close

Only use this close when you have a good rapport with your customer, otherwise he will get angry.

> 'Mr Jones, before you said that if you could afford it you'd like to have one, and doing it this way, you *can* afford it. (Now give him a big friendly smile.) You wouldn't lie to me, would you? – Congratulations, you've got a great deal!' (Stick out your hand.)

24 The Money to Throw Away Close

This close is for the very indecisive customer. It's more of an action close than a verbal one, and it uses pressure by dramatizing to the customer that he is throwing money away by not owning your (*product*). To implement this close you need to have three or four £5 notes, a waste paper basket and a roll of Sellotape. It works like this.

> 'Mr Jones, let me show you what you are doing every minute you delay your decision to own this (*product*). (Take out the £5 notes and say:) Now please feel free to stop me whenever you decide that you've thrown enough money away, and you're ready to start *saving* money!' (One by one, start to tear the £5 notes into little pieces and throw them into the waste paper basket. The majority of customers will be bemused with the first note, they begin to cringe and wince on the second and by the third note the pressure to stop you is unbearable so they blurt out 'OK, enough, I'll do it!' For the really stubborn ones who don't stop you, finish the close with:) 'I think I've proven the point that we're both throwing money

away, so let's stop it now this very moment. (Offer
your handshake and say:) Welcome aboard!' (I think
it's fairly obvious what the Sellotape is for.)

25 The Daydreamers, Ponderers and Go-Getters Close

'You know, Mr Jones, this world is made up of
three kinds of people: daydreamers, ponderers and
go-getters.
    'First, there are daydreamers, the dead legs, they
never achieve anything. Then there are ponderers,
they accept mediocrity and never try to better themselves. Finally, there are go-getters, the people who
stand out from the crowd, the achievers. Mr Jones,
I know which category you fall into, so don't let me
down, go for it.' (Hold out your hand.)

These next three closes should only be used when you have
a *very* good rapport with a customer.

26 The Uncertainty Close

'Mr Jones, I used to be just like you. I was always
so uncertain, I just couldn't make my mind up, I
was so indecisive. But now I am cured – now I'm
just not sure! (Pause.) Come on, Mr Jones, you know
that it makes sense, so give it a try?'

27 The 'Not for Everyone' Close

'Mr Jones, this (*product*) is not for upper-class people

and it's not for lower-class people, it's for middle-class people just like you and me. People who work hard for a living, people who appreciate the things they work for and people who deserve that little bit better. Mr Jones, I'm not going to let you walk away from this, not unless you tell me that you don't want it and I know you can't do that, so let's start the paperwork – now, what's your full address?'

28 The 'Walk Away' Close

This close can only be used when the sales situation is held on your home turf, not on neutral territory or the customer's turf. When the sales presentation is held in your home environment, the customer will feel obligation, especially when you have spent considerable time with him. The customer will not leave until he is, in effect, dismissed.

'Mr Jones I really don't feel that you could be silly enough to walk away from this (*product*) but if you can, there's the door. (Be very serious and don't pause or hesitate.) In fact, I'd like you to tell me honestly that this (*product*) doesn't make sense to you, that you don't like it and you don't want it. I'd like you to tell me honestly that you can't use it, that you can't see the benefits that it will give you and that you can't afford it! (Pause for two seconds – the customer will be too shocked to answer straight away, but if he does then it will be with the true objection.) Mr Jones, it makes too much sense, you can't walk away from it. Now, give it a try?'

29 The Secondary Issue Close

I like to call this close the 'David and Goliath' (the Boy
and the Giant). This close is an absolute classic and works
very simply, like this.

You pose the major issue but ask for a minor decision
– either way the customer answers, he has bought the
(*product*). The minor decision is always an alternative
choice. For example:

'It seems to me that the only real question now, is
how soon do you want to take delivery? By the way,
are you going to have it installed here in the office
or in the warehouse?'

or

'As I see it, it's going to be the deluxe version that
is best suited to you. (Pause.) Now, would you prefer
tea or coffee while we're doing the paperwork?'

or

'So, we've pretty much agreed that this (*product*)
would best suit your needs. By the way, would it
be better to take delivery tomorrow or Thursday?'

or

'As I see it, you would be better paying the policy
monthly by direct debit – or would you prefer to pay
annually?'

Whichever way the customer answers, he has bought. In
making the minor decision, the customer has also made

the major decision. Once the customer answers, he's closed, he's bought it – now all you have to do is say 'OK, let me write that down' and start the paperwork.

30 The 'I Want to Think About It' Close

This close is used when the customer says he wants to think about it. The phrase 'I want to think about it' is not an objection, it is an excuse, a leak, a statement consisting of a handful of words that basically means the customer is not ready yet. The customer doesn't want to say yes, but can't say no because he feels obligated and doesn't want to hurt the salesperson's feelings. (Obligated after using up so much of the salesperson's time.) The customer says he wants to think it over, to give himself some breathing space, to get himself out of the sales environment. If he is allowed 'off the hook' he will cool down – logic will set in and the customer will say to himself: 'Well, maybe next year, or I could always do this or that . . .' Any sense of obligation dwindles into non-existence, as does the chance of a sale.

The average salesperson dreads hearing 'I want to think about it', but a pro-clo looks forward to it because it means the sale is very near, the customer feels too much obligation, he feels too committed to simply say 'No, thanks'.

'I want to think about it' means 'Not yet, I'm not ready, I need more information, I need more convincing'.

To prove my point, imagine you go into a shoe shop to *buy* (not look at) a pair of shoes. As soon as you walk through the door a sales assistant comes straight up to you and says 'Can I help you?'. Without even thinking, the first thing that comes out of your mouth is what? . . . 'No, thanks, I'm just looking.'

Now, that doesn't mean 'No, I am not buying', it means
'Not yet, I'm not ready, I need to see something I like first,
I need more convincing'. 'I want to think about it' is not an
objection, it is an excuse. The 'I Want to Think About It'
Close will (every time) break down the excuse into a tan-
gible objection that you can overcome with another close.
     This is how the close works.

CUSTOMER: 'I want to think about it.'
PRO-CLO: 'OK, fine, so you're obviously interested
            then?'
CUSTOMER: 'I'm interested all right, but I just need
            some time to think things through.'
PRO-CLO: 'You're not just saying that, are you?'
CUSTOMER: 'No, of course not."
PRO-CLO: 'Well, to clarify my thinking, what exactly
            is it that you are not too sure about? Is
            it . . .' (It is imperative that you do not
            pause after asking the customer what he
            wants to think about, otherwise the cus-
            tomer will say 'Everything' and the close
            is lost.) 'Is it this benefit? Is it that benefit?
            Is it this benefit? Is it that benefit?'

You must go through the owner benefits without pausing
other than to let the customer say 'No' (it's not that).
     As you are running through the benefits, is it this?, is
it that?, if the customer doesn't give a tangible objection –
'Yes, that's it, that is what's concerning me' – you should
then conclude with:

PRO-CLO: 'It's the money, isn't it?'
CUSTOMER: 'Yes it is, that's the problem.'

The 'I Want to Think About It' Close never fails in

getting a tangible objection (usually money). Once you have a tangible objection, you should isolate it and then overcome it with another close.

31 The Summary Close

This close, as the name suggests, summarizes the product's benefits. It's a quick refresher course, to ensure the customer has understood everything, and to make sure the customer has enough product information and owner benefits to make the buying decision when asked to do so.

This is how the Summary Close works.

PRO-CLO: 'We agreed that the best-sized convervatory would be the 12 feet by 10, right?'

CUSTOMER: 'Right.'

PRO-CLO: 'And you prefer a dwarf wall to give you that warmer feeling, rather than having all glass?'

CUSTOMER: 'Yes'

PRO-CLO: 'We kind of agreed that it would be better to have the double glazing with three rather than two vents, didn't we?'

CUSTOMER: 'Yes, I think so.'

PRO-CLO: 'And the Victorian design is the one you're more biased towards?'

CUSTOMER: 'Definitely.'

PRO-CLO: 'And I'm sure that our special offer price, which in your case means that there is no charge for installation or construction of the base, is an appealing incentive to you, isn't it?'

CUSTOMER: 'Well, I guess so.'

PRO-CLO: 'Good, all I need now to set the wheels in

motion, is your OK, just here. (Hand the
pen to the customer.)

or

PRO-CLO: 'Mr Jones, you like this (*product*), don't
              you?'
CUSTOMER: (Just nods.)
PRO-CLO: 'And I know you can see the advantages
              and benefits of owning this (*product*), can't
              you?'
CUSTOMER: 'Well . . . yes, I suppose so.'
PRO-CLO: 'And if it were yours right now, you'd
              use it as well, wouldn't you?'
CUSTOMER: 'Yes, of course I would.'
PRO-CLO: 'So you like it, you want one, you'd use it
              and you can see the advantages of owning
              it – now, I know you can afford to do it,
              so Mr Jones . . . let's give it a try?' (Pop
              out your hand again.)

32 The Higher Authority Close

This close is most effective in the form of a take-away,
whereby you imply that there is no way, or very little
chance, that your manager or boss would approve whatever it is the customer wants. Of course, to be effective in
the first place, the customer must have a want or desire
for the product (it is impossible to close a door that hasn't
been opened).

The whole principle behind this close is to create a want,
a desire for the product and then deliberately take it away
by telling the customer he can't have it. This will have two
effects on the customer. First he will want the product

even more, and secondly, it will create the urgency to 'do it now'.

Here are a few variations on how the close works.

'Mr Jones, our absolute minimum deposit on this (*product*) would be £200. I can ask the manager if he will accept £50, but I don't think for one second he'd agree. (Pause.) But, if he did, would you take it today, or would you want us to deliver?'

'Mr Jones, I'm afraid that option isn't available to you, but if it were, if I could get it for you, would you take it?'

'Mr Jones, I'm sure the manager won't accept that offer, but out of professional courtesy, I'll put it to him. (Pause.) On the off-chance that he did accept it, would you be willing to go ahead?'

Once you receive a positive response from the customer, you should proceed in one of the following ways.

1   Do the paperwork first before seeking the approval of your higher authority, e.g. 'I'd have to show the manager what everything looks like on paper, but if he doesn't agree to it, we'll simply tear the paperwork up.'

2   Say to the customer: 'Well, as I said, I'm not sure we can do this, but . . . I'm going to stick my neck out, welcome aboard. (Handshake.) I'll just go and check.'

3   Leave the customer for a minute or two while you go and seek approval. (Go out of sight and hum the national anthem.)

Note: To keep the customer locked in and to maintain credibility, it is most important that you explain or justify your manager's approval. Let the customer think he got something really special – he'll love you for it!

33 The Reduce to the Ridiculous Close

This is a beautiful close that works exceptionally well when the customer is having a problem affording the money, or justifying spending the money. As with any close, for it to work the customer must be sold on the product – not just a whim, but a real desire.

The close works by breaking the money down to a ridiculously low amount and thus showing the customer that he can, in fact, afford it – in fact anyone can afford it. Let's see the close in action.

'Mr and Mrs Jones, £150 a month works out at only £2.46 each a day (£150 × 12 months ÷ 365 days ÷ 2 people = £2.46 each a day). That's only slightly more than the cost of a packet of cigarettes (if they smoke) or the cost of a couple of coffees each. (Pause.) For the price of a couple of coffees a day this (*product*) could be yours. Mr Jones, I know you can afford that, everyone can, so give it a try?'

(Remember to make the calculations on your calculator and show the customer the result in the window. See Step 21.)

The Reduce to the Ridiculous Close is also very effective when a customer is comparing the price of your product with that of a competitor's less expensive product. When this happens you should take the difference in price (only the difference) and reduce that amount to the ridiculous.

'Mr Jones, the difference (£3,000) in price when broken down over the next twelve months works out at £1.44 an hour. (Show the customer the calculator – £3,000 ÷ 52 weeks ÷ 40 hour week = £1.44 an hour.) Let me ask you this . . . Are you prepared to let £1.44 an hour stand in the way of increased quality production?'

Yet another use of the Reduce to the Ridiculous Close is when the pro-clo is trying to upgrade his customer from a small ticket item to a more expensive one.

'Mr Jones the deluxe version works out at an extra £16 a month, which is equivalent to only 52 pence a day! For 52 pence a day extra you can't not have it, can you?'

34 The Work Sheet (Order Form) Close

This close simply assumes that the customer is going to buy. You should move into this close in a smooth and easy flowing manner, there must be no pregnant pauses and no sudden movements. The Work Sheet (Order Form) Close evolves throughout the presentation in a natural way. If you become apprehensive or uneasy in assuming the sale, the customer will feel the same way and will not buy. The Order Form Close has to be implemented with the utmost confidence, but this one close can increase your earnings substantially, if you use it every time! So practise, practise, practise.

Here it is in action.

At the end of the presentation and after overcoming any basic objections, the pro-clo will say:

'Let's see what it looks like on paper. How do you spell the name of your street?' (This is a reflex question demanding a reflex answer – the question cannot be avoided. All you have to do is proceed to complete the paperwork.)

or

'I'd have to check to make sure we could get finance approval, so let's just see what everything looks like on paper. What's your full address, Mr Jones?' (Proceed to complete the order or finance form.)

or

'Would you prefer to take it in red or green?'
'Green.'
'OK, let me write that down. By the way what's your full address and telephone number?' (Proceed to complete the order form.)

If the customer allows you to fill in the order form he's bought, he's closed. But if the customer tries to stop you, it will almost certainly be with a real and final objection. Then you simply overcome the objection and continue with the paperwork as though it were the most natural thing in the world.

Once you have completed the order form, you should initial it yourself and then ask the customer to 'Just OK this, here, for me!' (handing a pen to the customer and indicating where he should sign).

35 The Sharp Angle Close (If I Could . . . ? Close)

The Sharp Angle Close works on the same techniques as the Echo Close, inasmuch as we throw the customer's positive statement or questions back to him, with a sharp, direct close.

Every time a customer makes a positive statement or asks a buying question, a pro-clo will use the Sharp Angle Close, every single time.

The difference between a sales representative and a pro-clo is that every time a sales rep hears a positive statement or a buying question, he will not close on it. Instead he will just agree with it, and in doing so the sales rep will gain nothing – he will not close the sale, he just waits for the customer to buy. For example:

CUSTOMER: 'I like that colour.'
SALES REP: 'Yes, it is nice.' (Nothing gained.)
PRO-CLO: 'Is that the colour you would like to have?' (A direct question.)

Instead of reaffirming a positive statement or simply answering yes to a positive or buying question, use the Sharp Angle Close, ask a direct question. Here are a few examples of the Sharp Angle Close in action.

CUSTOMER: 'Do you have any apartments on the ground floor?'
PRO-CLO: 'If I could find you one on the ground floor, would you have it?'

CUSTOMER: 'Can you do ten-year finance instead of five?'
PRO-CLO: 'If I could get you ten-year finance, would you be willing to go ahead?'

CUSTOMER: 'If we decide, could you have it here by
next Tuesday?'
PRO-CLO: 'If I could guarantee delivery next Tuesday,
can we do the paperwork today?'

Remember these five magic words: 'IF I COULD . . .
WOULD YOU . . . ?'

36 The Indecision Close

As the name suggests, this close is for the customer who
is indecisive. It works very simply like this.

PRO-CLO: 'Mr Jones, a great man once said (I use
Harold Macmillan): "Indecision has cost
more to the British public, British business and British government than wrong
decisions ever have." In essence, Mr Jones,
what we are talking about now is decision,
isn't it?' Whether to say yes or no and what
will happen if you say no or if you say yes.
'Well, if you say no, nothing will happen,
will it? But, if you say yes, these things
will happen. (Continue with a benefit
summary) . . . What do you *really* want
to happen, all these things or absolutely
nothing?'
CUSTOMER: 'Well, when you put it like that, of course
I'd like to have these things, but . . .'
PRO-CLO: 'Then give it a try?' (Hand outstretched.)

37 The Planting the Seed Close

This is a very powerful close, and to make it work you
must begin, not at the tail end, but at the front end of

your presentation, by implanting suggestion seeds in the customer's mind. These seeds will take hold and grow roots, so that at the end of the presentation the customer will feel that these suggestions or ideas are his own.

I disagree with the old saying 'You can lead a horse to water but you can't make him drink'. I believe if you make him thirsty (sell him), he'll drink!

Here are a few examples of how a pro-clo will 'plant the seed' at the front end of his sales presentation.

A 'Mr Jones, if you fitted UPVC double glazing, you would have the most attractive house in the neighbourhood.'

B 'The nicest apartments are the ones on the top floor, looking out to sea, don't you agree?'

C 'Investing in this bond gives you security and peace of mind, knowing your investment is safe.'

D 'Most people feel it's worth that little bit extra for this range, which is the most prestigious kitchen we do.'

Sometime afterwards, at the end of the sales presentation, once these ideas or thought seeds have had time to take root, it's time to close. For example:

A 'Remember how you said this would give you the most attractive house in the neighbourhood? I totally agree, so let's give it a go?'

B 'Remember you said it would be nice to have one looking out to the sea? Well, this one does . . . give it a try?'

C 'Mr Jones, remember you wanted the security of knowing that your investment would be safe? Well, they
don't come safer than this, and you get a very good
return, so let's go ahead?'

D 'Mr and Mrs Jones, do you remember that you said
you felt it was worth that little bit extra for the more
prestigious range? Well, I couldn't agree with you
more, and I think it would really make the kitchen
feel warm and inviting, so let's go for that one?'

38 The Worst Scenario Close

There is no question about it – a customer is always more
likely to get on board or get involved if he feels there is a
way out – an escape route (not a cooling-off period) in case
things don't work out. The idea behind the Worst Scenario
Close is to give the customer a sense of security, inasmuch
as he has a way out if the worst comes to the worst. The
customer is not tied, hook, line and sinker. His money is
not spent, gone for ever, it is invested wisely and will pay
him dividends, and of course at any time he likes he can
trade it in or swap it or cash it in or sell it, etc.

Depending on the product or service, the close
works something like this (I'll use double glazing as
an example).

'Mr Jones, let's look at the worst possible scenario.
The way I see it, the worst possible thing that could
happen is you'll end up with the most attractive house
in the area, and you'll make substantial savings on
your heating bills. The worst possible thing that could
happen is that you will never have to paint your
window frames ever again – from now on they're

maintenance free and almost completely soundproof. The worst possible thing that could happen is that you will dramatically increase the value of your home and make it a lot more desirable if you ever wish to sell it. Mr Jones, the worst possible thing that could happen is that, God forbid, you're made redundant and can't afford the payments – then the insurance, the payment protection plan, steps in and takes over the payments until you find a new job. You know, Mr Jones, with this (*product*) you have nothing to lose but everything to gain, so give it a try?'

In essence, the Worst Scenario Close is a benefit summary that is twisted around and manipulated to make the customer feel slightly intimidated into taking the plunge, but at the same time gives the customer a sense of security. (*Note:* I did not say false sense of security.)

39 The Silent Partner Close

On many occasions you will have a situation where one party is sold but the other isn't. The partner that is sold (usually the woman) remains quiet, whilst her partner airs his uncertainty. This close puts the unsold customer under pressure as he feels he's being ganged up on by the people he cares for (his loved one and his friend – you).

Here's how it works.

PRO-CLO: 'Mrs Jones, if this were your decision, if for some reason Mr Jones were not available, but you had his blessing – then based upon what you have seen and heard and on the information I've given you – you'd go ahead, wouldn't you?'

CUSTOMER: 'Yes, I would.'
PRO-CLO: 'Then, Mr Jones, for both of us and your-
                  self, give it a try?' (Hand outstretched.)

Occasionally, this close will start a family argument. If this
happens, you must take control and stop things getting out
of hand. You should tell your customers that it must be a
joint decision or none at all – then proceed with another
close directed mainly towards the unsold party.

40 The Kiss 'n' Tell Close

I call it that because the close is short and simple (KISS
it) and it tells the customer that now is the time to do it
(buy), not tomorrow.
   This close has a number of applications, but it's most
effective on the customer who puts up a lot of financial
resistance, or the younger customer who is just starting out in life. To implement the 'Kiss 'n' Tell' Close
you need to carry (either in your briefcase or in your
drawer) a pad of A4-sized paper.
   Let me explain.

'Mr Jones, let me use this pad of paper to demonstrate
a point to you. (Tear off a sheet of paper and fold
it in half three times so you end up with a small
rectangle.) Would you mind putting this piece of
paper in your pocket for me? (Hand the folded piece
of paper to the customer.) Now, Mr Jones, that
piece of paper is so small and light that you don't
feel it, even though you're aware that it's there.
In fact, after a little while you would completely
forget about it, wouldn't you?

(Then take a dozen or so sheets and fold them the same way.) 'Now, if I asked you to put this wad in your pocket, it would be a different story. This is bulky and you would feel its presence in your pocket all the time – it would be manageable but it would be uncomfortable.

(Finally, roll the entire pad into a tube shape.) 'And if I asked you to carry the whole pad, you couldn't, not without tearing the seams, because it's too big for your pocket! (Pause.)

'Mr Jones, I don't want you to take on something that's too big, or even something that's manageable but uncomfortable – I want to take the easiest option, I want you to get involved with this (*product*) without it being uncomfortable. The way I have proposed we go ahead, although you'd be aware of it for a day or two, after that you wouldn't even feel it, so give it a try?'

41 The Tape Measure Close

This close is more apt for the older or middle-aged customer – it is yet another close for the indecisive, 'I want to think about it' type. This will push him over!

'Mr Jones, you remind me of one of my clients who recently bought from me – like you, he was a little unsure about what he should do. Well, obviously in the end he got involved, but afterwards he told me what it was that prompted him to go ahead.

'He told me how he kept thinking about something his father had told him. That life is like a tape measure with each inch representing a year – and how very important it is to make full use of each inch before the tape measure runs out. He told me that in the past he'd let so many inches go by and he wondered how much of his own tape measure was left – that's when he decided to go ahead.

'Mr Jones, none of us know how many inches are left on our own tape measures. (Pause.) If you don't do this now you probably never will, so give it a try?'

42 Direct Closes

There are literally hundreds of ways of asking a customer to buy a product. However, a pro-clo doesn't ask a customer to 'BUY' it because that's asking the customer to COMMIT himself, in capital letters. Although a single word such as 'buy' would not stop a pro-clo from closing the sale, it is a word that should be avoided because it sounds very final and often threatening.

The pro-clo doesn't want his customers to feel they're buying it. They're not being pushed, they're not trapped for ever and a day, and he's not going to disappear overnight. The pro-clo uses words that are reassuring and customer-friendly, such as we, us, let's, etc. Here are some examples.

Do we have a deal?
Can you OK this for me . . . just here?
Can I have your approval today?
Can we go ahead?
Give it a try?
How about it, Mr Jones?
Should we write it up?
Let's do it?

The paperwork will only take a few minutes – welcome aboard!
Do you want it?
If I could . . . would you join us today?
Can I have your order now?

Remember the golden rule: once you've asked the question, you stay silent and remain that way until the customer responds.

43 The Lion Heart Close

So-called because you must be brave and have nerves of steel to use this close. The technique is very simple – you agree with everything the customer says, and in doing so you put yourself under pressure. Pressure to respond, to justify, to overcome. This is where the nerves of steel come in, because you must resist this pressure and sit tight – the customer will then feel awkward and either back down or justify what he has said. For example:

CUSTOMER: 'It's very expensive.'
PRO-CLO: 'Yes, it is.' (Silence.)

The customer will then either back down and say something like 'But I suppose it's worth it', or he will justify what he has said: 'It's a little bit out of my price range.' Either way, the pro-clo can then go in for the kill.
   Here are a few more examples. Put yourself in the customer's position and see how you would react to the closer's response.

CUSTOMER: 'I don't like the colour.'
PRO-CLO: 'Ummmmm!'

CUSTOMER: 'I didn't come here to buy.'
PRO-CLO: 'I know . . .'

Lion hearts are big pussy cats, so to finish off with, how about a nice 'lay down' (pun intended) and roll over?

CUSTOMER: 'Could you just run through the figures one more time?'
PRO-CLO: 'Certainly . . .'

44 The Handshake Close

When the battle has been going on for a while and you have used close after close but don't seem to be getting very far – then try this one. You'll be amazed by the results.

> Act defeated, shrug your shoulders, smile and say: 'Mr Jones, I'd like to just shake your hand.' Offer him your hand, and when he takes it say: 'Congratulations, you've made a wise choice. Now, would you like a drink while we're doing the paperwork?'

This simple, direct, straight to the point close will throw the customer off balance, and he will react in one of two ways. Either he will buy, or he will give you a final objection. Try it!

45 The Pick of the Bunch Close

This close is for the confused customer who is unable to

make up his mind because he's got too many options in front of him.

Whenever this situation occurs, you must take control and, using the process of elimination, narrow the options down to only two. You must explain to the customer why each option is not suitable for him and then eliminate it by taking it away from the table. (Out of sight is out of mind.)

When there are only two options left, ask the customer which of the two he is more biased towards and when he chooses one, simply stick out your hand and say: 'I agree with you, welcome aboard!'

46 The Saving Money Close

This one is a very simple close, using plain old common sense. It basically tells the customer to stop beating about the bush and to get on with it.

Here's an example.

PRO-CLO: 'Mr Jones, I'm sure you'd agree that everyone is interested in saving money, right?'

CUSTOMER: 'Yes, of course.'

PRO-CLO: 'So let me ask you, when do you think is the best time to start saving money – now, or next year, or maybe the year after that?'

CUSTOMER: 'Well, when you put it that way . . .'

PRO-CLO: 'There is no other way to put it, Mr Jones. If you want to save money on this (*product*), then you should get on board right now, so come one, let's give it a try.'

47 The Silence Is Golden Close

This close is for use straight after you've just asked them to give it a try – that's right, straight after. Read on.

Earlier in this book I explained about the pressure of silence (Step 36), and how important it is to stay silent after you've asked the customer a closing question. For fear of contradicting myself, I must make it clear that this close is for very, very occasional use – only when your perception tells you that the silence of pressure is having an adverse effect. (Maybe the customer is shaking a little.) You use this close to bring a little warmth or humour into the situation and relax the customer slightly, by easing the pressure – but only slightly.

Smile warmly with your eyes and say:

'Mr Jones, they say that "Silence is golden" and I agree – how about you?'

Then remain silent again, with a confident warm smile, and nod slightly. As soon as the customer nods in agreement, or says 'Yes, I suppose so', stick out your paw.

48 The Investment Close

This is another close used to suggest that the customer should save money by doing it now. It intimates that the customer would be silly to hesitate or let this offer pass by.

It works like this.

'Mr Jones, imagine you had an opportunity to join a scheme that would save you, say, 10 per cent of your mortgage every month – you'd jump at the

chance to join, wouldn't you? Well that is, in effect, what I'm offering you now, a chance to get
on board at below the going rate and guaranteeing
that you will save money in the future – so give it a
try?'

49 The Referral Close

Most companies nowadays run a referral programme,
whereby a customer is rewarded for supplying referrals, or
quality leads, that get converted into sales. Normally, the
reward or incentive is money or goods to the value of.

The referral close is used when the customer has a
problem with the monthly repayments. Alternatively, if
the product is a small ticket item and the customer pays
cash, the referral close can be used as an additional owner
benefit to close the sale.

This one works like this.

PRO-CLO: 'Mr Jones, if I owed you £1 for every friend,
relative, neighbour and work colleague you
know, how much do you reckon I would
owe you in total?'

CUSTOMER: 'I don't know . . . maybe £150 or £200.'

PRO-CLO: 'Mrs Jones, if I owed you the same, how
much do you reckon I'd have to pay you?'

CUSTOMER: 'Probably the same."

PRO-CLO: 'And I bet if I paid you £10 for everyone
you knew, you would go out and meet more
people, wouldn't you?'

CUSTOMER: 'You bet we would.'

PRO-CLO: 'Well, over the years we've found that our
best form of advertising is by word of
mouth or recommendations from satisfied

customers. This has proved to be so effective that we (*company*) pay (*£50*) for each referral that also decides to purchase from us. That means that if you gave us just two referrals a month and they bought, then your monthly repayment is taken care of. Now I know from what you just told me, you could find at least two recommendations a month to buy one of these (*product*), couldn't you?'

CUSTOMER: 'Easily.'

PRO-CLO: 'Then let's give it a try?'

You should proceed to have the customer write down as many referrals (names and addresses) as he can – these are great quality leads and are money in the bank for everyone.

You should show the customer how, by sending in referrals that get converted, he will not only have his monthly repayments taken care of but will end up with money in his pocket too. 'Just think, you could end up with this (*product*) for free and be paid for doing it as well.'

Crazy world, this selling game!

50 The 'Treat Yourself' Close

This is a close for the customer who is deliberating over a luxury item or maybe some accessories that are not a necessity to the performance of your (*product*). For the best results you should become a little passionate (not sexually) towards the end.

PRO-CLO: 'Mr Jones, supposing you walked into your building society and they started giving money away to the first people who queued up. Whereabouts in that queue would you like to be?'

CUSTOMER: 'Right at the front, of course!'

PRO-CLO: 'You'd want to treat yourself to as much as you could get, wouldn't you?'

CUSTOMER: 'Absolutely.'

PRO-CLO: (Time for a little passion in the voice.) 'You know, Mr Jones, you work hard week in and week out, grafting away to pay the bills and support your family. Now I ask you, don't you think you deserve to jump to the front of the queue every once in a while and treat yourself to something a little special, like this (*product*). Well I think you deserve it, so go on, Mr Jones, treat yourself!'

51 The 'Pedal as You Go' Close

This is another close for the customer who is being a little pig-headed because he can't afford the one he really wants, or the customer who doesn't like the idea of taking finance but can't afford to pay for it all at once. The idea is to make the customer feel that it's quite normal to take it in stages and he can progress as quickly as he likes.

Here we go.

'Mr Jones, very few people get involved straight away with (*the deluxe model*), most start with (*the standard*) and then upgrade at a later date. It's like learning to ride a bike, you don't just jump on and start pedalling straight away. First of all, you start with a tricycle, then when you get used to pedalling and steering you progress to the bicycle, and then if you want to go all the way, you carry on to the unicycle. It's a natural progression. And it's much the same with this (*product*). You should get involved now with this (*option*) and then pedal as you go. That's the only way to do it, isn't it? Right, so climb on board!' (Offer handshake.)

52 The Emotion vs Logic Close

When your customer is still looking for justification to go ahead, try this one.

'Mr Jones, all buying decisions are made either emotionally or logically. Let me explain. When we *need* something, we make a logical decision to buy it. And our decision, our investment, pays dividends because we've satisfied our needs. On the other hand, when we *want* something, we make an emotional decision, but that too pays dividends because then we've satisfied our wants.

'Well, Mr Jones, this (*product*) is for you logically, because you know it makes sense and will save you money, and emotionally, because of the pleasure and satisfaction you will derive from it. You will in fact benefit from twice as many dividends – so give it a try?'

53 The De-Pressure Close

This is a very clever little close, used when the customer says 'You're pressuring me'. The first thing you must do is cool off – go out of the woods, go around the trees, and then pop back into the woods again.

It is worthwhile noting that a pro-clo very rarely has the customer say that he feels pressured, because a pro-clo knows how to pull not *push!*

Listen to the close in action.

CUSTOMER: 'You're pressuring me.'

PRO-CLO: 'I'm sorry, I don't want you to think that . . . it's just, I'm so enthusiastic about this (*product*) and I'm so convinced it would work for you, that I may have got a little carried away.

'Mr Jones, to clarify my thinking, let's just quickly recap over a few of the points we've covered.

'You were happy with this (*benefit*) weren't you?

'And you were happy with that (*benefit*) as well?

'We also agreed that . . . didn't we?

'And correct me if I'm wrong, but we felt that this one would be the best option, didn't we?

'Well, Mr Jones, we've covered everything and you said yourself you were happy, so . . . give it a try?'

If the customer says 'You're doing it again', then do it again, but with a different approach.

PRO-CLO: 'Mr Jones, supposing I was to find out that you were about to make a big mistake that would cost you bundles of money. Would you rather I told you about it before or after it happened?'

CUSTOMER: 'Of course I'd rather you told me before.'

PRO-CLO: 'That's just what I've been trying to do, stop you from making a big mistake. I don't want to see you throwing money away, so let's do something about it right now, what do you say?' (Raise your eyebrows and nod gently.)

54 The Decision vs Choice Close

This is a close for the timid customer who is not able to make the decision without a gentle tug at his sleeve. This close simply manipulates the customer's words and gets him to close himself. (It takes a little practice.)

PRO-CLO: 'Mr Jones, you wouldn't have wasted your time or mine going through this presentation if you weren't genuinely interested, would you?'

CUSTOMER: 'No, I wouldn't.'

PRO-CLO: 'So the way I see it – you'd like to have this (*product*), that decision is already made. Now it's just a choice – whether you should put it off and run the risk of losing it, or paying more for it in the future . . . or whether you should get involved now at the right price and the right time. (Pause.) Mr Jones, why don't you give it a try?'

If it doesn't work, take it a step further and try this, a little stronger this time:

PRO-CLO: 'Mr Jones, you've just told me that you are seriously interested. Nobody would put off and be willing to pay more for something in

the future if they were that interested. You
wouldn't lie to me, would you?'

CUSTOMER: 'No, I wouldn't!'

PRO-CLO: 'Then give it a try?'

55 The 'Proof Is in the Pudding' Close

A pro-clo always has numerous closing tools at his disposal, something for every occasion such as testimonials,
letters of credibility, graphs, charts, maybe a previous
customer, and so on. The 'Proof Is in the Pudding' Close
works by using one or more of these tools actually to
close the sale. Some groundwork has to be laid down
to use this close successfully, inasmuch as you must make
the customer feel the odds are stacked in his favour.

The best way to illustrate this, as always, is by way of
example.

PRO-CLO: 'Mr Jones, I'm pretty certain that one of
              the things that is bothering you is whether
              or not you can get a better (*deal*) at So-
              and-So's. Am I right?' (Create your own
              objection.)

CUSTOMER: 'Well I must admit, that is one of the
              things.'

PRO-CLO: 'If I could prove to you right now, be-
              yond any shadow of a doubt, that this is
              the best (*deal*) you can get, would you go
              ahead today and give it a try?'

If the pro-clo is successful in making the customer feel
confident that the odds are in his favour, the customer
will readily agree. All the pro-clo has to do then is to use
his tools, prove it, and then say:

PRO-CLO: 'So, there you have it, but the real proof is in tasting the pudding. Now (taking out the order sheet), what is your full address?'

As with every other close in this book, this close can be adapted to any product or service. The trick is to create an objection that you know full well you can overcome.

56 The Take-Away Close

Another close that evolves from the take-away principle. This one uses reverse psychology – instead of you selling the customer, the roles reverse and the customer ends up selling (his eligibility) to you. In plain English, this close creates the emotion of greed, or fear of losing out.

Here are some examples.

'We (*company*) are only looking for one house in this area to use as a show house. I know it would mean a substantial saving to you but, I'm just not sure whether this would be the right street for us. I don't know if we would get the right exposure!'

'Mr Jones, I know that's the best one but I really don't think you'd be able to manage it, I think it just might be out of your league.'

'Mr Jones, I don't think we should waste any more of each other's time. I really don't know whether or not we could get finance approval – so why don't we fill out the forms and see if you'd be eligible?'

Mr Jones, you can't have that one (*product*), they're

for our existing customers or people who need something slightly smaller.'

The customer will then start to justify or sell himself, he
will try to convince you that he, the customer, is eligible
to buy.

Once you've been sufficiently convinced, you should
turn round to the customer and say:

'OK, you've convinced me, I'm prepared to let you
have it. Welcome aboard.' (Hand outstretched.)

With this close the customer is made to feel special, he feels
that he's getting a good deal. One thing is for certain, there
are very, very few cancellations from this close.

57 The Drop Close

Price them high, you can always come down, but price them
low and you've got nowhere to go.

Every salesperson sells products that have different
prices. You should always endeavour to sell a higher-priced
item whenever possible, so that you've got somewhere to
manoeuvre to if you find you're flogging a dead horse.

The Drop Close has two applications.

1   When all other objections have been eliminated but
     the customer still can't decide. When you know you're
     hitting your head against a brick wall and you're losing
     him.

2   When the customer just can't afford the propo-
     sal you've put to him (being a condition, not an
     objection).

The Drop Close creates fresh blood. It is a very effective
close and will stimulate the customer's excitement again,
as he feels he's getting a better deal.

Here are the examples.

'Mr Jones, how about if you just take one now and
I could give you a ninety-day option to get the
second one at the same price? If I could do that,
would you be willing to go ahead?'

'Mr Jones, if I could get you a smaller model that
would do exactly the same job, but it was 20 per
cent cheaper, would you take it?'

'Mr Jones, if I could knock off enough to pay for
(*whatever*), would you shake my hand?'

'Mr Jones, instead of taking the full 5,000, how
about if we split the container and you just take
3,000 now?'

Remember, any sale is better than no sale at all, and once
you're in the door, it is always so much easier to sell them
some more.

58 The Testimonial File Close

This is not so much a close you should say, but rather
a close you should do – one that will speak for itself.
You should create a testimonial file and collate together
as much material as you can, things like photographs of
happy owners or any celebrities who own your product, letters from satisfied customers, credibility literature

from solicitors, accountants, doctors, and so on. Also things like newspaper clippings, write-ups about your industry, and photocopies of purchase agreements from previous sales. You should update this material regularly, and keep your testimonial file with you at all times because it's worth a fortune to you.

Customers follow the crowd, they have what is called the herd instinct, and where one goes the others will follow. If you can show your customer that this path has been trodden before, by someone from the same 'herd', the likelihood of his doing the same is greatly increased.

I once knew a salesperson who used this close with every customer and he achieved amazing results. He didn't have one testimonial file, he had two, but the contents of each were identical.

Every time he made a sale he would photocopy the agreement twice and put a copy in each file. In one file all the agreements were in alphabetical order under town and then street. In the other file they were all in alphabetical order under the customer's occupation – accountant, builder, carpenter, etc.

Whenever he was with a customer he would show them his files and ask them if they knew So-and-So, from Such a Street. Then he would show his customers all the other, say, plumbers who had bought from him. He had well over 1,000 contracts in each file and every customer found someone he either knew or could relate to.

When it was time to close the sale, the salesperson would pick up these two files, one in each hand, and he would say to his customer: 'You can't tell me that all these people were wrong . . . so let's join them!' More than a few of them did just that!

59 The 'Before I Go' Close

When all else fails, when you've tried close after close after close, maybe ten times or more, but to no avail, then you should give up, accept defeat, and try this one.

PRO-CLO: 'OK, Mr Jones, I know when I'm beaten. I accept defeat reluctantly, because I'm convinced you should own this (*product*) but nevertheless, I know you're not going to buy.' (Start to clear away your things, prepare to leave and the customer will relax visibly.)

'Before I go, is there any chance you could help me with something?'

CUSTOMER: 'Well, I'll try. What is it?' (The customer will readily agree because he feels embarrassed and guilty and a little obligated after using up so much of your time.)

PRO-CLO: 'Do you know of anyone else locally who you feel might be interested in my *(product)*?'

CUSTOMER: 'Well, let me see . . . there's So-and-So next door, they need a new one.'

PRO-CLO: 'That's great! (Write down the details.) Anyone else?'

CUSTOMER: 'Yeah, there's Bob at work, he needed one, and then you could try . . .' (Write them all down, these leads will keep you busy for a while. When the names and addresses start to dry up, interrupt the customer . . .)

PRO-CLO: 'Hang on a second! There's something funny going on here!'

CUSTOMER: 'What makes you say that?'

PRO-CLO: 'You've just given me the names and

addresses of five people, friends and neighbours, who you think will benefit from my (*product*). You're saying that it's good enough for them but not for you – I don't believe it, Mr Jones. Come on now, what is it that's really stopping you?'

The customer will give you the reason or the final objection, and hey presto, you're back in the ball game again.

60 The Apology Close

This is the last close in this chapter because it is the last close that you should use before calling it a day.

This last shred of hope, this very last close, should be used on every single customer, because in doing so you will close an extra 5 per cent – an extra one in twenty.

The Apology Close works because the customer thinks he's off the hook, his guard comes down and all of a sudden he's vulnerable again.

The trick is sincerity – this is how it works.

'Mr Jones, I know you're not going to buy and I have to accept that, but I've done a lousy job and I'd like to apologize because I feel as though I've let you down. (Don't hesitate or allow yourself to be interrupted.) You know, I don't think I have ever met anyone this (*product*) is more suitable for. Would you just do me one last thing, so that I don't ever make the same mistake again? Tell me, what was it that stopped you from going ahead?'

Again, because the customer feels a little awkward, guilty, embarrassed, or obligated, he will tell you the reason for not purchasing or he'll give you the final objection. Either way, you're back in again for another close.

I've known customers to say things like 'This is not really my wife', or 'We lied about the deposit, we just couldn't have afforded it', or 'We didn't like to say, but we put a deposit on one yesterday with a competitor' – stuff that is easy to turn around again.

PART FOUR

Your Shop Opens
After You Close

Avoiding Buyer's Remorse

The sale begins after the close, not before.

A pro-clo starts work when he receives an objection, a 'no', but he doesn't *really* start work until he receives a 'yes'. The pro-clo understands that once he has closed the sale, if it is to complete, he must start selling, not stop selling. (Understand that the pro-clo doesn't start selling the product again, but rather he sells himself again and he sells his company's back-up and after-sale service.)

The customer must never be allowed to feel that the pro-clo was just out for what he could get (his commission). The customer must not feel that now the pro-clo has got what he wants he has, all of a sudden, lost interest and wants to be somewhere else. When this happens, and a customer feels he is going to be dropped like a tonne of bricks, there is obviously a strong likelihood he will cancel.

A qualified prospect may have an interest in the product but very, very few intend to buy there and then. The pro-clo creates a need or a desire, he involves the customer and gets him excited, then he closes the sale when the customer is emotionally at the highest point. When the customer comes down again, back to earth as it were, the regret often seeps in.

Over the next few pages we shall look in detail at the procedure the pro-clo follows to keep the sale sold and avoid buyer's remorse.

Congratulate and Compliment

The customer has now agreed to purchase, but in many cases he is still somewhat uncertain and apprehensive and maybe a little nervous. This is a very important time and it is critical that the salesperson behaves properly. The customer is waiting to see what happens next, and he is watching the salesperson so see if he becomes overexcited, to see if maybe he misjudged, or to see if the salesperson develops a 'take the money and run' attitude. Now, more than ever, the customer needs that friendly, warm and sincere arm of reassurance around him, to help him through these troubled times.

Immediately upon achieving the sale, the pro-clo will shake hands and congratulate his customer. Remember that actions speak louder than words, and shaking hands is the accepted gentleman's way of cementing an agreement. Once the customer has accepted the outstretched hand, it would then be ungentlemanly (or unladylike) to change his mind or back down. Psychologically, when he accepts the handshake he accepts the decision to go ahead.

Whilst shaking hands, the pro-clo will congratulate his customer and compliment him on his wise decision. Here are a couple of examples.

'Congratulations, John . . . you've certainly got an eye for quality and I know you're going to really enjoy your new (*product*).'

'Congratulations and welcome aboard . . . you've made a wise decision. This is not only going to make you the envy of all your neighbours but it will greatly increase the value of your home.'

Filling in the Forms

So many salespeople are incompetent when it comes down to filling in the forms – so much so that *many* a sale has been lost due to mistakes, or uncertainty and sheer incompetence. These salespeople often work hard to close a sale, only to lose it again because they haven't learnt how to do the paperwork. They are so close, yet so far away.

A pro-clo knows his paperwork inside out, he is so conversant that he can complete an agreement or work sheet in a matter of seconds. A pro-clo practises until he is an expert, until he can complete the paperwork with his eyes closed.

The salespeople that have to concentrate on the paperwork (because they haven't bothered to learn how to do it) are normally very quiet whilst they are writing. This silence can easily cause anxiety in the customer, and he may (because it's quiet and he has time to reflect) say to himself 'What am I doing?'. Then all the doubts and fears come streaming back. When this happens, the salesperson might try for another half-hour or so to get the deal back in, but in most cases it's lost for ever.

The pro-clo already knows most of the information needed to fill in his forms, but still he involves the customer by confirming what he already knows. As he writes, the pro-clo continues with light conversation to keep things running smoothly and to make the customer feel comfortable with his decision. The pro-clo acts as if completing the paperwork were the most natural thing in the world, and his light conversation is often completely unrelated to the product. The pro-clo might talk about the customer's work or family or hobby – anything that takes the customer's mind off buying and demonstrates that he is not just interested in the customer's money.

Cementing the Deal

To guard against possible cancellations, the pro-clo will prevent, as much as possible, what is termed buyer's remorse. Once the paperwork has been completed or typed and has been approved (signed), it's time to cement the deal, to button it up, to reassure the customer that he has done the right thing. This will make him feel somewhat obligated to go through with it, to complete.

Here are the six steps that the pro-clo follows once the deal is signed and sealed.

1   *Say thank you*
     This is one of those little things that separates the pro-clo from the masses. Saying thank you costs nothing but means a lot, and is remembered. Very few salespeople bother to thank their customers, which is one of the reasons they get more than a few cancellations and less than a few referrals. When you thank a customer sincerely, he will warm to you and he will want to offer you something in return, he will feel obligation. Consider this example.

     'Mr Jones, I'd just like to say thank you and tell you that I'm grateful for your custom. If you ever need me for anything at all, I want you to know that I'm here for you. I don't want you to be a one-time customer, I want you to be a life-time customer, so don't ever be afraid or hesitate to call me.'

     When a customer hears this, he knows he's made the right decision and he is grateful for your reassurance and your friendship. When he knows that *he* won't be let down, how can he change his mind and let *you* down?

2   *Give them possession*
The sooner the customer takes ownership, the better. Whether your customer is to receive a service, or whether he is to take delivery or collect, or whether you are to arrange installation, get it done as soon as possible – that means immediately. Once the customer experiences ownership, when he tastes the benefits and sees the results, he won't dream of changing his mind.

3   *Go the extra mile*
Give your customer that little extra, the unexpected something, the icing on top of the cake. Just like the baker who gives his regular customers thirteen cakes instead of twelve (a baker's dozen) – it's good business. Your customer feels he's got a good deal and again he feels obligation or, put another way, he feels loyalty.

4   *Seek out referrals*
Customers are the most excited immediately after they have purchased. It stands to reason, then, that now is the time when the customers will be the most receptive to offering referral leads. You should ask your customers if they know of anyone else who might be interested and whether they would mind you using their name. If you persevere gently, they will always give you one or two referrals – but if they seem reluctant, don't beat it to death, leave it for another time.

These referrals should be followed up the same day or the following day, while the customer is still hot. This, again, makes the customer obligated to go through with the deal. After all, he can hardly recommend other people and then not go through with it himself, can he?

5   *Treat them*
As a token of your appreciation, a gesture of friendship and goodwill, treat your customers. Buy them a present. Here, it's the thought that counts, not the monetary value. The gift could be a box of chocolates, a bunch of flowers, a bottle of wine, or maybe a meal. On the other hand, the treat could be in the form of a commitment from you, e.g. a round of golf or a trip to the theatre with yourself and your spouse. In a nutshell, accepting a gift creates an obligation to remain a customer, especially when buyer's remorse pays a visit. Remember, every penny spent is worth a pound!

6   *Send them a note*
Many customers suffer a bout of buyer's remorse when it's time to pay. Whether it's the full payment or the first instalment, it is likely to be sometime down the road, not there and then when they agree to purchase. A nice little touch is to send them a note or a letter or a card to compliment and thank them once again.

This not only serves as a gentle reminder of their commitment, but also they will recall how they feel for you and Mr Obligation pops his head up again. Your note should be short and sweet and handwritten – this conveys the message of it being personal and warm instead of official or threatening. One final point: make sure they receive your note two or three days before payment day, but don't mention money.

Here's an example.

Dear John and Mary,
    Just a quick note to say congratulations once again and to welcome you as valued customers.

It really was a pleasure meeting you both and I'm looking forward to seeing you again soon, but in the meantime please remember that if you need me for anything at all, you only have to call. Again, congratulations and thank you for your custom.

My regards and best wishes,
A. Pro-clo

A true pro-clo doesn't just 'sell 'em and forget 'em' – he keeps in touch regularly with his customers and they get SERVICE, in capital letters . . . which leads us on to our last technique.

Make hay while the sun shines

It is a fact that the easiest and cheapest source of new business is from existing customers. A pro-clo knows this and so he is forever in contact with and servicing his existing customers. The truth is, they don't get the chance to forget about him and they wouldn't even consider purchasing from somebody else.

Every owner of your product is a potential source of additional sales, referrals and testimonials, not just once, but continuously, year after year. Over a period of time, a pro-clo will build a very sizeable clientele who provide referrals. This creates a snowball effect, and his owners list keeps growing and growing. This source of business is so lucrative that many a pro-clo will work only off his owners list and yet earn a very substantial living. Remember, it's easier, cheaper and continuous, and every owner is a potential source for additional sales, referrals and testimonials. As well as that, the closing ratio is *at least* 50 per cent – which means that as you progress in this profession you don't work harder, you work smarter – and it's a lot more rewarding.

Additional Sales

Why is it that so many salespeople are satisfied with making one sale to one customer? The answer is that they lack foresight and simply aren't hungry enough. Once you have made a sale and your foot is in the door, so to speak, it becomes so much easier to tag on.

Every single product or service anywhere can be sold in duplicate, every product or service can be upgraded to a bigger, better and more expensive one. For that matter, every product or service can be downgraded, but then of course you add on, to make it worthwhile. No matter what you sell, you will have accessories or other related products, and most of the time you only have to make the owner aware that they are available – and he will want to buy.

To illustrate, consider how many times you've walked into a shop, for example a newsagent's to buy a newspaper. As you stand at the counter to pay for the newspaper you notice the confectionery on display. (This is called point of sale advertising – the shopkeeper tries to make his customers aware of other products.) You only wanted a newspaper, but how many times have you bought (impulsively) a bar of chocolate or a packet of mints?

Don't be satisfied with one sale, go back in, time and time again. But remember – the key to repeat business is SERVICE.

Referrals

Learning how to canvass referral business was covered in detail on pages 64 (Step 13), 235 (The Referral Close) and 246 (The 'Before I Go' Close). For an owner to continue supplying referral leads, it is very important that you do not neglect to thank him. Regardless of whether or not the referral purchases, the pro-clo will write a thank you note to his owner (existing customer), or pay him a call, or at the very least telephone him to let him know the outcome and thank him.

Testimonials

A prospective customer will always feel that the closer is somewhat biased, but seeing is believing, and the credibility behind an endorsement from a satisfied owner is second to none. Testimonials are so effective that some companies and organizations spend hundreds of thousands of pounds on using famous celebrities to promote and advertise their products via television, radio and the press. Yes, a testimonial is a very powerful selling and closing tool!

A pro-clo, because he provides SERVICE, receives testimonials – but he doesn't necessarily wait for them to arrive of their own accord, because he knows that most customers, although they are happy, very rarely get around to expressing their happiness and gratitude on paper. A pro-clo solicits and collects testimonials from his satisfied owners, he uses a highlighter pen to emphasize the important parts of each letter, and slowly but surely he builds up such an array that he has a testimonial to overcome every doubt or concern or objection he might hear from a future customer.

Asking an owner for a testimonial letter is like asking a friend for a reference – most are very flattered and are only too pleased to repay the compliment. The way to get the best kind of testimonials is to simply ask your owner for his honest and down-to-earth opinion of you, your product and your company. Then ask if he wouldn't mind doing you a favour and put it in writing. He will.

Remember, once you've closed the sale, keep selling. Follow the six steps to avoid buyer's remorse.

1 Say thank you.

2 Give them possession immediately.

3 Go the extra mile.

4 Seek out referral business.

5 Treat them.

6 Write to them.

Finally, remember that every one of your owners, your existing customers, will buy more, will supply you with referrals and testimonials, if you provide SERVICE – if you follow up and follow through.

Go get 'em, pro-clo!

If your would like to contact
the author, please write to

Ian Seymour
c/o Pelican Publishing Company, Inc.
1101 Monroe Street
Gretna, Louisiana 70053

Book List

Henzell-Thomas, Nigel, *Supercharge Your Selling* (London: Hutchinson Business, n.d.).

Hopkins, Tom, *How to Master the Art of Selling Anything* (London: HarperCollins, 1983).

LeBoeuf, Michael, *How to Win Customers and Keep Them For Life* (London: Piatkus, 1991).

Lewis, Dr David, *The Secret Language of Success* (London: Corgi, 1991).

Peale, Norman Vincent, *The Power of Positive Thinking* (London: Cedar, 1990).

Trisler, Hank, *No Bull Selling* (Hollywood, Fa: Fell, 1988).

Ziglar, Zig, *Zig Ziglar's Secrets of Closing the Sale* (New York: Berkeley, 1985).

Index